# EVERYDAY INSTRUCTIONAL COACHING

### Seven Daily Drivers to Support
### Teacher Effectiveness

# Nathan D. Lang-Raad

Solution Tree | Press
a division of
Solution Tree

555 North Morton Street
Bloomington, IN 47404
800.733.6786 (toll free) / 812.336.7700
FAX: 812.336.7790

email: info@SolutionTree.com
SolutionTree.com

Visit **go.SolutionTree.com/instruction** to download the free reproducibles in this book.

Printed in the United States of America

Library of Congress Cataloging-in-Publication Data
Names: Lang, Nathan D., author.
Title: Everyday instructional coaching : seven daily drivers to support
    teacher effectiveness / Nathan D. Lang.
Description: Bloomington, IN : Solution Tree Press, [2018] | Includes
    bibliographical references and index.
Identifiers: LCCN 2017046574 | ISBN 9781945349485 (perfect bound)
Subjects: LCSH: Mentoring in education. | Teachers--In-service training. |
    Teachers--Training of.
Classification: LCC LB1731.4 .L36 2018 | DDC 371.102--dc23 LC record available at https://
lccn.loc.gov/2017046574

**Solution Tree**
Jeffrey C. Jones, CEO
Edmund M. Ackerman, President

**Solution Tree Press**
*President and Publisher:* Douglas M. Rife
*Editorial Director:* Sarah Payne-Mills
*Art Director:* Rian Anderson
*Managing Production Editor:* Kendra Slayton
*Senior Production Editor:* Tara Perkins
*Senior Editor:* Amy Rubenstein
*Copy Editor:* Jessi Finn
*Proofreader:* Evie Madsen
*Cover Designer:* Rian Anderson

I'd like to thank my fiancé Herbie Raad. Your love, passion for writing, quick wit, creativity, boldness, sense of humor, and wisdom inspire me to be my best. You continually tell me how proud you are of me, and that's the only affirmation I'll ever need in life. I dedicate this book to you. I love you.

# ACKNOWLEDGMENTS

I would like to thank Tim Kanold, who first inspired me to become an author and share my experiences with the world. You have positively influenced me by your friendship and mentorship. Thank you for always listening and encouraging me.

I'd also like to thank Douglas Rife, who afforded me the opportunity to write about one of my passions. I appreciate the support and encouragement you have given me over the years.

Solution Tree Press would like to thank the following reviewers:

Jamie Ackart
Assistant Principal
Shoal Creek Elementary School
Kansas City, Missouri

Charlenee Hardee
Instructional Coach
Memorial 9th Grade Academy
Port Arthur, Texas

Elita Driskill
Coach/Consultant
ESC Region 11
White Settlement, Texas

Clint Heitz
Instructional Coach
Bettendorf High School
Bettendorf, Iowa

Liisa Gilbert
Instructional Coach
Chaska High School and La Academia
Chaska, Minnesota

Thelma Holmes
Reading Instructional Coach
Ridgegate Elementary School
Houston, Texas

Catherine Gokey
Instructional Coach
Robert E. Lee Elementary School
Grand Prairie, Texas

Diana Lee
Instructional Coach
Downtown Magnets High School
Los Angeles, California

Sandra Meador
Instructional Coach
Rose Hill Elementary School
Alexandria, Virginia

Judi Sprung
Instructional Coach
Willmar Public Schools
Willmar, Minnesota

Lauren Smith
Instructional Coach
Noble Crossing Elementary School
Noblesville, Indiana

Nakoa Wiley
Instructional Coach
Whitefoord Elementary School
Atlanta, Georgia

Visit **go.SolutionTree.com/instruction** to
download the free reproducibles in this book.

# TABLE OF CONTENTS

# ABOUT THE AUTHOR

 **Nathan D. Lang-Raad, EdD,** is a speaker, author, and professional learning facilitator. He is chief education officer at WeVideo. Throughout his career, he has served as a teacher, assistant principal, university adjunct professor, consultant, and education strategist. He was director of elementary curriculum and instruction for Metropolitan Nashville Public Schools, as well as education supervisor at NASA's Johnson Space Center. He speaks at both local and national professional conferences. He is the cofounder of Bammy Award–nominated #LeadUpChat, an educational leadership professional learning network (PLN) on Twitter. Nathan is also the cofounder of #divergED, a Twitter chat focused on divergent thinking and innovations in education. He is a Google Certified Educator, Microsoft Innovative Educator, and 2016 Apple Teacher and serves on the Children's Right to Read International Literacy Association Task Force.

Nathan has written several blog posts featured on the EdTech K–12, Corwin Connect, Education Week, K–12 Blueprint, and Solution Tree websites.

Nathan received a bachelor of arts in general science-chemistry from Harding University in Searcy, Arkansas, a master of education in administration and supervision from the University of Houston-Victoria, and a doctorate of education in learning organizations and strategic change from David Lipscomb University in Nashville, Tennessee.

To learn more about Nathan's work, visit http://nathandlang.com or follow @nalang1 on Twitter.

To book Nathan D. Lang-Raad for professional development, contact pd@SolutionTree.com.

# INTRODUCTION

In the ever-changing landscape of education, now more than ever before, schools need instructional coaches who know how to support teachers and students through varied teaching and learning challenges. Although instructional coaching isn't brand-new, ambiguity still exists around the role of an instructional coach. The crux of instructional coaching should be a daily, intentional, and purposeful engagement with all learners in the school community to support teaching and learning in innovative and transformational ways. Instructional coaches need their own supports to determine how to fulfill this function each day. As instructional coaching expert Jim Knight (2007) states, coaching is "one of the most unpredictable professions in education; each day brings surprises, new challenges, and successes" (p. 19).

As we embark on the journey of instructional coaching, we must identify drivers that will not only support the work of an instructional coach but also aid in transforming the role of instructional coach in the same way classrooms are being transformed. You might ask, "Shouldn't I just follow a coaching framework, prescriptive model, or cycle?" While instructional coaching frameworks, models, and cycles are helpful for defining the overall work of an instructional coach, we live in a dynamically changing educational context that is often unpredictable and that requires innovative approaches daily. Classrooms are being transformed into learning studios, libraries into learning commons, and brick-and-mortar schools into virtual learning spaces. Teacher professional learning is on demand, self-directed, and personalized. Teachers access, deliver, and facilitate content, curriculum, and instruction in various blended online and off-line media. Students are expected to develop skills to solve local and global problems that have yet to arise, and become the next generation of leaders and entrepreneurs. All these conditions, and more, require that instructional coaches know how to quickly determine how to best support teacher effectiveness throughout changes in education. The *drivers* presented in this book provide foundational guidance that helps drive this action because they are not framed inside a rigid structure or in a prescriptive fashion the way frameworks, models, and cycles often are. The works and research of Adam Grant (2014), Carol Dweck (2007), Susan Cain (2012), and Don Beck and Christopher Cowan (1996) also provide new insights into how people live, work, collaborate, and view the world.

Based on these changing demands and this emerging information, I've identified a set of seven drivers for effective daily instructional coaching—catalysts that will support and guide coaches through this ever-changing educational landscape.

1. Collaboration

2. Transparency

3. Inquiry

4. Discourse

5. Reverberation

6. Sincerity

7. Influence

Coaches can create a sense of inspiration, compassion, empowerment, and empathy around instructional coaching when they apply these drivers on a daily basis. These daily drivers work to produce successful outcomes not only for coaches but also for principals, teachers, students, and parents.

## About This Book

This book explores the seven drivers of instructional coaching to build on, refine, and innovate ways that instructional coaches work and communicate with teachers. These drivers will help illuminate the importance of the teacher's role in student learning, and the importance of instruction.

Chapter 1 explores the driver of collaboration. Coaches should share their expertise, practices, and purposes daily while embracing diversity and dissonance among the educators they serve. They can lead the development of a school community in which collaboration with all learners makes coaching an expectation and a safe, normal, and critical part of the teaching profession and the school and district culture. Chapter 2 dives into the driver of transparency. Coaches hear a lot about creating buy-in and trust. There is no better way for coaches to genuinely create trusting, positive, and collegial environments than to establish a culture of transparency about their intentions, their goals, and even their own flaws and mistakes in teaching and learning. Once coaches create a culture of transparency, they can begin to implement the driver of inquiry by asking questions with the purpose of changing the cycle of thinking and learning, which is the focus of chapter 3. Chapter 4 concentrates on the driver of discourse—the art of purposefully choosing language norms to convey that coaches value all stakeholders as people and value their ideas and perspectives. Chapter 5 centers on a driver that I call *reverberation*: a meaningful two-way oscillation of feedback that coaches fuel with trusting relationships and consistent dialogue. Coaches push themselves to become the best versions of themselves and encourage teachers to do the same through the instructional coaching driver of sincerity, the focus of chapter 6. And finally, chapter 7 explores the driver of influence, through which coaches can catalyze change efforts in education.

Throughout these chapters, I will draw on powerful and groundbreaking conclusions of the latest research on growth mindsets from Dweck (2007), communication from Cain (2012), and sociocultural psychology from Grant (2014), which all lend support to the efficacy of the seven daily drivers. I will share daily behaviors, practices, and tools that help define the role of an instructional coach. Reproducible tools appear throughout the book to guide readers and offer opportunities to reflect on new learning, explore new ideas, and create actions that immediately put new learning into practice. Visit **go.SolutionTree .com/instruction** to download the free reproducibles in this book.

## About the Coach's Role

This book is for everyday instructional coaches, ranging from novice to veteran. The seven drivers can transform any instructional coaching or leadership capacity. An important underlying concept of this book is that coaches need to act on the seven daily drivers with humility. They must not get caught up in the official title or status of the instructional coach; they should instead focus on the unprecedented support they will provide to teachers using the drivers. Dacher Keltner, Deborah H. Gruenfeld, and Cameron Anderson (2003) explain that people who boldly claim status inside an organization are not the ones who most readily and reliably attain and hold power; the best leaders lead from behind the scenes, not loudly out in front. Additionally, while people often perceive personality (especially extroversion) to be a crucial factor in leadership efficacy, Corinne Bendersky and Neha Shah (2013) find, "Whereas personality may inform status expectations through perceptions of competence when [teams] first form, as group members work together interdependently over time, actual contributions to the [team] are an important basis for reallocating status" (p. 387).

The seven drivers connect instructional coaching concepts to quantifiable actions that work to make a difference in how coaches support teachers. Each driver will help provide direction and energy to our daily practice and journey as instructional coaches. Each chapter highlights a driver and contains instructional coaching stories, illustrations, tools, and connections to research in education and psychology. Some suggestions in this book challenge the status quo of instructional coaching, which I've observed as including an undefined function of supporting teachers with limited resources, support, and leadership. The drivers in this book build on time-tested research and on the latest psychology research to help inspire actions that transform the coaching role. I encourage you to deeply reflect throughout each chapter, apply the ideas to your own coaching context, and ask yourself what might be holding you back from implementing innovative solutions to improve teaching and learning.

# ONE

# COLLABORATION

Coaches can establish a diverse, inclusive, purposeful, and collaborative community when they take the temperature of the school climate and invite people who have differing views to the table.

Dismissive responses to attempts at collaboration arise all too commonly in schools. Take, for instance, the teacher who walks into a team meeting ready to create a vision with her teammates and is met with cynical team members who say, "I don't have time for that right now." The teammates also give nonverbal cues that they are too busy; after all, they have papers to grade, copies to make, and preparations to complete for the next day. Consider also the instructional coach who brings her ingenious idea to the principal, who meets her with an impassive attitude because the principal feels overwhelmed with his to-do list of managerial tasks. Additionally, imagine the district leader who has experienced success in trying something new and different and shares the strategy with the district instructional team, which turns down the idea immediately, saying it is not scalable and, therefore, would not work at a systems level.

Coaches often meet heavy resistance to collaboration because their schools have had an impermeable culture of continuing with practices that "work," without questioning their validity, even when circumstances have changed. Lack of collaboration quickly leads schools to extinguish ideas or prevent people from ever sharing their ideas in the first place. When this happens, urgency, creativity, and zeal at best occur in small pockets but will not exist at an organizational level. Collaborative malpractice transcends the school building and permeates other aspects of the organizational leadership structure.

It's easy to shift the blame for collaborative malpractice to the school build-ing's culture, mandate overload, or lack of time, but a hard look in the mir-ror could reveal something surprising. We all contribute to a noncollaborative culture when we continue to only respond to urgent requests and react to the multitude of tasks required of us. Always prioritizing the actions that allow us to simply cross things off the required to-do list takes away more and more collaborative opportunities. Instead of having teachers spend all their energy on trying to cross more off their mandated to-do list each day, schools should empower teachers to take innovative risks and invest in creating connections and relationships.

Teachers and instructional coaches must venture into new and unexplored territories in order to create highly functioning, creative, and impactful teams. Essentially, I am asking coaches to transform collaboration in a way that breaks traditional molds by promoting diversity, embracing dissonance, and ensur-ing balance. Coaches who value and act on diversity and inclusion and who encourage divergent ways of thinking while nurturing trust and accountability will begin to produce the outcomes required to positively change the landscape of teaching and learning. Coaches have a unique opportunity to influence the culture and context of their school. Their inherently consultative role affords them the freedom and flexibility to approach their work differently. This chapter will explore strategies instructional coaches can use to promote diversity within collaboration, leverage dissonance to strengthen collaborative outcomes, and balance social interactions within collaboration.

## Diversity

We often think of diversity as relating to demographics, but experiences based on race, gender, age, and so on may not necessarily be the only kind of diversity that is important for the coach-teacher team dynamic to learn from. Diversity also encompasses a range of educational roles, ideas, perspectives, and instruc-tional approaches. Creating diverse environments is important not only because it helps build stronger communities and organizations but also because diver-sity impacts the way our brains function. A study comparing diverse groups to more homogeneous groups finds that diverse groups demonstrate higher levels of innovation, creativity, and problem solving than less diverse groups (Phillips, Mannix, Neale, & Gruenfeld, 2004). Diverse groups outperform more homo-geneous groups not only because they bring an influx of new ideas but because diversity prompts team members to process information differently and to con-sider different ways of working (Phillips et al., 2004). According to research-ers Katherine W. Phillips, Elizabeth A. Mannix, Margaret Ann Neale, and Deborah H. Gruenfeld (2004), even though people often feel more comfortable with others who are like them, like-mindedness hinders the exchange of different ideas and the intellectual processes that arise from disagreements. Generally, people prefer to spend time with other agreeable people. But this unchecked affirmation does not always produce productivity and problem solving. Facing unfamiliarity takes more cognitive processing because it demands conflict resolution and emotional-energy expenditure. Through this cognitive struggle, new ideas emerge, and people learn from one another in unexpected ways and discover new solutions.

If we recognize that diversity builds stronger collaborative thinking and innovation, why do schools have difficulty addressing diversity in working relationships? I would argue the answer to this question has to do with the fact that when emotions and dissenting opinions mix together, acting on decisions becomes more complex and time consuming. Additionally, because teachers are already strapped for time, it seems more efficient for them to sync up with the teacher friend next door who will validate their opinion or practice. Teachers find comfort in sharing with a colleague who shares their beliefs. However, when we choose to surround ourselves only with those who agree with us or who reinforce or validate our beliefs, rather than those with diverse experiences and opinions, we develop an *implicit bias.*

According to Ohio State University's Kirwan Institute for the Study of Race and Ethnicity (2015):

> Implicit bias refers to the attitudes or stereotypes that affect our understanding, actions, and decisions in an unconscious manner. These biases, which encompass both favorable and unfavorable assessments, are activated involuntarily and without an individual's awareness or intentional control.

Whether we like to admit it, implicit bias is pervasive and affects every person connected to a school, no matter how open-minded educators think they are, or how diverse their team has tried to become (Staats, 2016). One example of implicit bias is that people tend to believe others more if they have an accent similar to their own (Lev-Ari & Keysar, 2010). Educators can possess implicit bias toward students who speak differently or colleagues who have a different accent. As you think about that statement, reflect on your own attitudes and actions toward people who speak with the same accent as you, and your attitudes toward people who speak with different accents. Also honestly evaluate your perceptions of anyone who might speak with a different tone, display differing personality traits, or approach conversations differently.

Implicit biases also have an enormous impact on both our own personal behavior and coach-teacher relationships. It impacts the decisions we make about student potential and student behavior correction, and our perception of colleagues' credibility or competence. The great news is that research does conclude we can take purposeful steps to create inclusive teams. In *Everyday Bias*, Howard Ross (2014) provides a framework of systems and structures that illuminate bias patterns and provide remedies to address them to promote an open exchange of diverse ideas within teams.

Ross (2014) provides a strategy using the mnemonic PAUSE.

- **P:** Pay attention to what's actually happening beneath the judgments and assessments.

- **A:** Acknowledge your own reactions, interpretations, and judgments.

- **U:** Understand the other reactions, interpretations, and judgments that may be possible.

- **S:** Search for the most constructive, empowering, or productive way to deal with the situation.

- **E:** Execute your action plan.

Consider a scenario in which you have a coaching conversation with a teacher and he or she exhibits less eye contact than you prefer. Let's *pause* and think through what's really happening. (See figure 1.1.)

| |
|---|
| **P:** The other person exhibits little eye contact. What's actually happening is the other person doesn't look me in the eye for the same amount of time I look others in the eye. |
| **A:** My initial interpretation is the other person possesses low self-esteem or self-confidence. |
| **U:** Is this person intimidated by my body language or my use of eye contact? Does this person simply prefer to communicate without sustained eye contact? Does this person have a different cultural background? |
| **S:** In this scenario, I'll continue to speak in a friendly and casual tone, staying cognizant of my eye contact and varying the duration of my eye contact to ensure the other person feels comfortable with displaying the body language that fits the conversation. |
| **E:** I will continue to get to know the person and develop a relationship of trust and transparency, taking note if the eye contact changes. |

**Figure 1.1: PAUSE sample scenario.**

Using the PAUSE strategy encourages a coach to look at all the possibilities to help disarm immediate conclusions. In the eye-contact example, PAUSE can help the person re-evaluate assumptions (*Should I assume the person lacks confidence because his or her eye contact doesn't meet my personal standards?*) and chosen responses (*Should I get to know this person a little better before I make an assessment? How should I engage this person in the future?*). By illuminating our natural inclinations when working with others and making proactive changes in our actions, we can truly build a collaborative culture where everyone wins.

Besides the PAUSE strategy, coaches have three additional actions they can take to address bias head-on and proactively engage diversity.

1. **Create a list of unstructured processes, and structure them:** What activities do you do that don't align with a specific purpose or process? Consider, for example, the teachers you engage with daily. How did you make the decision to focus on those teachers? Are they your friends? Do you have pleasant and comfortable interactions with them? Do you primarily interact with the predominant ethnic group in the school? Do you tend to give more praise to certain teachers, regardless of the evidence you collect? Also consider your feedback system. Have you structured it to align with previously established goals, or have you based it on your own presuppositions about teachers?

   Once you develop your list of unstructured processes, create an unbiased structure. Ensure your daily interactions include all teachers. Create feedback processes that align with co-created goals. (See chapter 5, page 49, for more about feedback.) Structure allows us to make sure that all teachers have opportunities to be nurtured, embraced, and successful and to grow.

2. **Engage with teachers who are different from you:** As noted earlier, *diversity* does not only refer to demographics. *Different from you* means more than just race, gender, sexual orientation, and so on. It also includes thinking style and personality. Although a coach is expected to work with all teachers, undoubtedly, coaches may tend to favor having more frequent interactions with teachers who are more like them. As our schools become more diverse, so will (or should) our faculty. Personally and professionally, I have observed that the more we get to know someone, the more differences we become familiar with and even embrace subconsciously.

3. **Encourage others with opposing viewpoints to speak out:** Dissenters and devil's advocates can often frustrate us, especially when we are pushing our own ideas or ways of working. Organizational change often gets pushed through by those teachers who speak the loudest and who talk over those with opposing viewpoints. But if coaches preach to challenge the status quo in

education, they must listen to and act on well-reasoned dissonance and criticism from teachers. Which teachers disagree with you or often try to derail your efforts? Give those teachers the opportunity to reason through their thinking by having thoughtful, reflective dialogues in a safe environment. This encourages collaboration through embracing diverse ideas and freely giving trust. (For more on dissonance, see the next section beginning on this page.)

Of course, schools must also address diversity in recruiting, hiring, and onboarding practices. In his book *Originals*, psychologist Adam Grant (2016) advises organizational leaders seeking to build more innovative and successful organizational cultures to hire for cultural contribution rather than cultural fit by actively seeking diversity in experiences, skills, and personality traits, rather than hiring those who think in similar ways. To ensure diversity, coaches must take part in the hiring decisions made by leadership. These practices foster dissonance that can lead to collaborative strength.

## Dissonance

Dissonance occurs when some elements of collaboration don't seem to work in concert with one another. It can damage collaboration if not harnessed in the right way. In an attempt to foster collaboration, principals often ask their coaches to facilitate collaborative common planning to discuss standards, normed assessments, and instructional strategies. Oftentimes, this looks like a rushed gathering focused more on logistics than on strategies. Although it's appropriate to ensure we stay productive, we should utilize our collaboration time in the most meaningful way. This valuable face-to-face time together provides opportunities to create goals, discuss strategy (for example, personalizing learning), and articulate progress. A culture of collaboration is only possible when all teachers feel affirmed as educators and valued as contributing members of the team. However, this does not mean that coaches should aim to eliminate all dissonance. In fact, some forms of dissonance can actually be beneficial.

When working with existing faculty, how can coaches champion dissonance when visioning, creating new ideas, and monitoring growth? Grant (2016) suggests identifying the person who commonly acts as a loyal opponent or devil's advocate, instead of randomly assigning someone a devil's advocate role, because the assignment becomes just that: a role one plays. If the identified person doesn't truly have a passionate feeling for or against an idea, he or she won't have a compelling argument, and the argument won't truly represent an opposing viewpoint. Dissonance must be authentic so that emotion and experience translate to thoughtful communication of ideas.

A school building contains plenty of opinions to harness. We should look not to create opinion bash fests but to leverage dissonance in a way that leads to purposeful change in teaching and learning. Coaches can discover where dissonance exists in their school through the use of a survey that contains statements meant to invoke emotion or reaction. Figure 1.2 features sample responses to a list of dissonance-discovering prompts that coaches can pose to teachers and have teachers answer anonymously or in confidence.

| |
|---|
| **Directions:** Respond to each of the following prompts. |
| I differ from many of my colleagues in how I (pick one or more of the following actions or create your own): decide on curricular resources, implement technology, utilize instructional strategies, plan for instruction, or create assessments in the following ways.<br><br>*Implement technology: I first begin with the behaviors and learning dispositions required for students to be successful outside the classroom. Then, I decide what technology tool would help achieve this goal. I don't implement a tool just because it's the latest and greatest tech tool.* |
| Other teachers would be surprised to know that:<br><br>*I believe teaching is exhausting. I love it and am called to do it, but it's a relentless profession that requires a lot of hard work and energy. My continual expression of positivity and gregariousness is deliberate and hard at times.* |
| I wish my principal would do, say, or act on:<br><br>*I wish my principal would come in my classroom more and give me feedback. The occasional walkthroughs feel like she just needs to check a box.* |
| I wish my coach would do, say, or act on:<br><br>*I wish my coach would provide me with some more strategies and support. Sometimes I feel stuck or just in a rut and need a boost from some fresh ideas or perspective.* |
| My students think I'm an effective teacher because I:<br><br>*I'm effective because I laugh a lot and make class fun. I also genuinely care about them as students and as future leaders.* |
| If I could change one thing about education, it would be:<br><br>*If I could change one thing, it would be that I would receive more trust as a teacher. Sometimes I feel like the next initiative is to make me comply with a mandate aimed to make me better, but in the end creates frustration and additional work.* |

**Figure 1.2: Dissonance-discovering prompts.**

*Visit **go.SolutionTree.com/instruction** for a free reproducible version of this figure.*

After teachers respond to these prompts, compelling statements, outlandish ideas, and dissenting opinions can emerge. This process gives teachers an outlet to share their expertise, practices, and purposes transparently and frequently. Coaches, in a sense, take a cultural pulse and invite people who have differing views to the table. After receiving these responses, coaches are able to leverage dissonance by acting on teachers' specific desires and wishes. We, as coaches and school leaders, oftentimes do a really great job collecting copious amounts of assessment data or listening to the latest education buzz, but we frequently struggle with using the data to change our practice. It takes courage and perseverance to act on the information we discover and allow those who hold different viewpoints to take the microphone.

## Balance

While collaboration is important, having team members collaborate excessively and not allowing them time to think and work independently leads to danger. Further, collaboration may cater to certain personality types over others. For these reasons, coaches must carefully ensure balance when working with teachers in a collaborative setting. Coaches can begin to understand how to strike this balance by examining the concepts of groupthink and introversion versus extroversion, considering a variety of balancing methods they can incorporate into their practice, and following three important principles of working as a team.

### Groupthink

*Collaboration* is most definitely in your repertoire of educational jargon, but *groupthink* probably isn't. *Groupthink* refers to the conformity that results when a group of people come together. This phenomenon, for example, is present in a study by psychologists Jamil Zaki and Kevin N. Ochsner (2012), in which fMRI scanners measured brain activity and identified that if an individual views a photo of someone with a group of people, and the group expresses that it finds the person in the photo attractive, the individual will consider the person in the photo more attractive than he or she would have without that group. Zaki and Ochsner (2012) find that the reward networks of the human brain respond to the photo of the person after it has gained exposure to the positive judgments of fellow group members, which can lead to the conformity present in groupthink. Coaches, however, have an opportunity to facilitate collaboration in a way that doesn't lead to groupthink. It's crucial that coaches actively honor individuality within the group and create opportunities for teacher teams to work together in effective ways through collegial-focused (as opposed to groupthink) tools that I'll continue to provide throughout this book.

## Introversion Versus Extroversion

The TED Talk *The Power of Introverts* (Cain, 2012) and book *Quiet: The Power of Introverts in a World That Can't Stop Talking* (Cain, 2013) have received a great deal of attention for challenging and criticizing schools and notable businesses and organizations for overvaluing extroversion and primarily creating work environments that cater to extroverts. Susan Cain (2013) examines personality types in relation to social stimulation instead of to the often-interpreted *shy versus not shy* comparison. According to Cain (2012), "Extroverts really crave large amounts of stimulation, whereas introverts feel at their most alive and their most switched-on and their most capable when they're in quieter, more low-key environments."

Cain (2012) tells a story about Steve Wozniak, cofounder of Apple. Because of his popularity and his work with Steve Jobs, you might initially think Wozniak's success resulted from a collaborative approach to creativity or his work in highly social workplaces. As it turns out, his success did not result from a big, open-concept space full of huddling brainstormers plotting their course on whiteboard walls. Cain (2012) describes how Wozniak always made progress by himself on his journey to build the first personal computer (PC). Wozniak made much of this progress in his cubicle at Hewlett-Packard. He'd arrive really early in the morning before any of his colleagues to read engineering magazines, pore over technical manuals, and come up with designs in his head. After work, he'd quickly have dinner at home and then drive back to the office to have a late night of work. Cain (2013) notes, "He describes this period of quiet midnights and solitary sunrises as 'the biggest high ever'" (p. 73). The key, then, to capitalizing on our talents and skills is for us all—introverts and extroverts and those in between—"to put ourselves in the zone of stimulation that is right for us" (Cain, 2012). This means allowing time for teachers to work independently as well as in collaboration.

Grant (2014) finds that "introverted leaders often deliver better outcomes than extroverts do, because when they are managing proactive employees, they're much more likely to let those employees run with their ideas," whereas extroverts get so enthusiastic about their team's ideas, they unconsciously start taking credit and "putting their own stamp on things" (as cited in Cain, 2012). This extroverted leadership keeps other team members' ideas from gaining traction or even being illuminated. Applying this conclusion to the coach-teacher relationship, coaches can leverage the team's great ideas by facilitating collaborative work that empowers teachers to be innovative instead of imparting their knowledge onto teachers.

I'm not proposing we stop collaborating together as teams, nor would Cain (2012, 2013) suggest that. The overwhelming culture of schools and society continues to shift more and more toward teamwork and collaboration. More than ever, learning should be part of a social context, as learners collectively rely on each other's thinking to solve complex problems.

What I am proposing is we not allow the pendulum of collaboration to swing to the far extreme of cooperative learning all the time, promoting excessive group work and overly social norms in the classroom. Like in the classroom, I also suggest a balance of healthy collaboration in teacher teams. Cain's (2012, 2013) and Grant's 2014 research on introversion and extroversion is compelling, and we must address how coaches can work most effectively and creatively with all personality types by creating balance.

## Methods to Ensure Balance

Coaches are facilitators of collaboration and therefore can ensure a creative environment that balances social stimulation. Based on my observations and experiences, I have identified the following three key actions that will support coaches' efforts toward balanced collaboration.

1. **Create a casual, fun, and relaxed environment:** With the important work required of teachers and the pressures they often face, following this principle carries more weight than ever before. Sharing ideas and discussing learning standards and instructional strategies are pertinent for this environment. But when it comes time for creation and critical thinking, don't force everyone to execute these cognitive functions in a formal environment. This concept segues into the next key action.

2. **Provide structured quiet time:** Remember nap time for students? Well, we're not quite going there, but we must utilize quiet time in an intentional way. Quiet time is best for reflection, contemplation, and creation. Quiet time can also mean alone time, depending on what your team members need. If you carve out an hour of time with your team, and your objectives for that meeting require complex thinking or creation, set aside at least thirty minutes for quiet time. A possible breakdown of this hour could look like the following.

   ‣ Establish objectives for collaboration. (Five minutes)

   ‣ Set the stage for problem solving, ask clarifying questions, share thoughts, and so on. (Ten minutes)

- Have quiet time for reflection, productive work, and creation. (Thirty minutes)

- Debrief quiet time, and share work with teammates. (Ten minutes)

- Conduct a closing circle to discuss next steps, actions to take, and responsibilities. (Five minutes)

3. **Identify and share personality types:** Coaches can find many assessments online, such as Myers-Briggs Type Indicator (www .mbtionline.com), CliftonStrengths (www.gallupstrengthscenter .com), and so on, that can help them decide on the best way to assess and illuminate personality types and strengths. Not only is this beneficial for advocating balanced collaborative processes, but it will also be pivotal in working one-on-one alongside teachers. Once teachers share their personality profiles in a trusting environment, you'll begin to sense mutual understanding and respect among team members. We will fully utilize quiet time when we make connections between how we work best and how that intersects with our interactions with others.

In addition to the practical methods coaches can use to strike the right balance in their collaborative practices, coaches should also consider principles that will help keep their collaborative work on track.

## Principles of Working as a Team

Obstacles like groupthink, one-size-fits-all collaboration, extroverted learning environments, and unconscious bias can quickly derail educators' important work if they don't have a set of guiding principles they can frequently turn to. When working with collaborative teams, I'm often reminded of a sport that only enters the limelight during the Olympic Winter Games: curling. Curling is a sport that, at first glance, makes you say to yourself, "They are sliding a stone across ice. How is that an Olympic sport? And what's up with all of the screaming and the crazy-looking sweeper mops?" But after you watch a match, you learn to appreciate the value of this unique game. To succeed at curling, curlers must have three principles in place.

1. **Focus:** The gentlest touch of a stone can have a huge effect on the stone's trajectory. It takes extreme focus and concentration for curlers to ensure they place a stone on a path to eventually land on its target.

2. **Teamwork:** All of the screaming that occurs is how players communicate with each other. A high level of strategy and teamwork goes into choosing the ideal trajectory and placement of a stone. Everyone has an important role in the game and must do his or her part in order for the team to successfully execute the play.

3. **Peripheral vision:** With the teammates' laser focus on the stone, it's amazing that nobody kicks a stone while sweeping. Curlers not only have a laser focus on the path of the stone but also possess excellent peripheral vision to make sure they avoid any obstacle (a player or a broom) that could alter the path of the stone.

Instructional coaches apply these principles to how they plan, collaborate, and execute their "plays." Even while coaches remain extremely focused on the eventual goal and outcome, they must simultaneously stay on the lookout for potential obstacles in their periphery. Our actions must be truly focused and aligned with our vision.

## Conclusion

Truly collaborative coaches are shining examples of how to champion diversity in our learning spaces, making teachers feel accepted, inspired, and supported. Additionally, many teachers and administrators tap successful coaches for knowledge and lean on them heavily as instructional experts, but in school cultures that continue to react to the urgent instead of prioritizing the important, their expertise often goes untapped.

Effective collaborative coaches don't shy away from dissonance but take advantage of it as a natural process of promoting positive change. Good collaborative coaches don't push their own opinions as the best advice but simply and humbly seek better ways of teaching and learning. Accordingly, they surround themselves with a diverse group of people with different experiences and thoughts in hopes of gaining new perspectives and new knowledge. *Lifelong learning* is more than just a catchy phrase to them; they live it out with purpose.

It takes a team of people with diverse talents and skills, and opportunities to dissent, for positive growth and development to occur and for the team's plan to remain on the ideal trajectory.

# TWO

# TRANSPARENCY

Coaches are able to create trusting, positive, and sharing environments when they are transparent about their intentions, their goals, and even their own flaws and mistakes in teaching.

Instructional coaches start off at a disadvantage in some ways when teachers associate the coach's role with change at the classroom level. Even inside a positive culture, if people think you, as a coach, might be attempting change to the structure of norms, defenses go up. But if teachers work in a climate where they feel coaches are trying to help them and learn alongside them, and when coaches transparently share their own flaws and weaknesses in teaching, teachers will open up to their coaches. Teachers will then want to listen and even welcome you with open arms. Author Simon Sinek (2009) articulates the connection between transparency and collaboration by making the distinction that a team is not just a group of people who work together but a group of people who trust each other. And trust can only exist through transparency.

Transparency drives action because it allows all stakeholders to drop their defenses and be palpably honest in their current understanding and practice. It advocates full disclosure and trust, which helps remove some of the most difficult barriers in communication and team culture. This chapter explores the transparency concept of *naked service*, offers a tool to help gauge transparency levels, and provides strategies to develop greater transparency with teachers.

## Naked Service

In a culture of unconventionally high levels of transparency that enable us to redefine and rewrite the legacy and role of impactful teaching, everything is up for questioning, and nothing is off-limits. This higher echelon of transparency encourages principals, coaches, and teachers to quickly share failures and mishaps as often as they would want to share kudos and wins. Teachers have the ability to vocalize challenges in the classroom so they may receive support from coaches to help students achieve success. Everyone wins in this new realm of transparency. We must acknowledge, however, that this kind of transparency also requires a great deal of trust from all stakeholders due to the vulnerability this level of sharing creates.

Author Patrick Lencioni (2010) coined the term *naked service* to describe the vulnerability a service provider should have with its clients and customers. Lencioni's work has helped leaders and their teams create thriving organizations, and their collective achievements reveal that by having complete transparency and vulnerability with their clients, leaders can build radical levels of trust and loyalty that far surpass anything they have previously experienced. Uniquely, this degree of service questions the traditional approach of service providers, trying to convince their customers that they know all the right answers and that they don't make mistakes. Customers find this "perfect" persona inauthentic and often manipulative.

Why do people resist being transparent? They resist because of fear. Lencioni (2010) specifies three fears that, if not addressed, create barriers against trust, loyalty, and transparency between organizations and their customers.

1. **Fear of losing the business:** Organizations can be so hyperfocused on not losing customers or money that they develop a fear that thwarts them from engaging in challenging conversations with their clients. Even though a difficult conversation may cause some initial discomfort, the outcome develops loyalty and trust. Clients want assurances that the mission of an organization encompasses a desire to meet the clients' needs more than to protect the organization's revenue streams.

2. **Fear of being embarrassed:** It's disconcerting to publicly make mistakes or have failures exposed in front of others. This fear keeps service providers from sharing their mistakes because of a perceived notion of needing to be right or perfect. Naked-service providers proactively ask questions and make bold statements even at the risk of getting proven wrong or exposing an area of weakness. Clients develop trust in service providers when the service providers conquer this fear and demonstrate that they will not hold back their ideas or mask failures for the sake of appearing flawless.

3. **Fear of feeling inferior:** In this context, Lencioni (2010) sources the fear of feeling inferior as more rooted in social and emotional perceptions than in intellectual ones (like the fear of being embarrassed). Naked-service providers focus on doing what the client needs rather than just trying to be important to the client.

How do Lencioni's findings relate to instructional coaches' work with teachers? Coaches are like the service providers, as they meet the needs of their clients (in this case, teachers). Teachers become the recipients of support and services to meet their needs (such as instructional support, learning-environment support, and so on).

We can recontextualize the fear of losing business as a fear of losing likability in the context of coaches. Coaches desire to become trusted confidants; therefore, they consider likability an important factor. However, if coaches don't overcome this fear, they will not have the difficult conversations necessary to establish meaningful relationships or provide helpful feedback for professional growth. Instructional coaching expert and University of Kansas professor Jim Knight (2010) frames this concept concisely in his book *Unmistakable Impact*, stating, "When teachers stop learning, so do students" (p. 4). The work of a coach is not for the faint of heart, as coaches must learn, implement, and master new teaching practices and engage in transparent conversations about what works and what doesn't.

We can directly connect the fears of being embarrassed and feeling inferior to the coach-teacher relationship as well. Because of the perceived role of the instructional coach as a master teacher, coaches may place an unnecessary burden on themselves to appear to have expertise in all aspects of teaching. Although I'm being tongue-in-cheek here, these are very real fears, and even though we may hear that our job as coaches is to work alongside teachers to illuminate strengths and identify growth opportunities, we can't help but give credence to these fears and question ourselves. *What if the teacher learns that I've never taught that grade or subject? What if the teacher finds out I wasn't a reading specialist? What if the teacher finds out I'm not a mathematician?*

But don't teachers have these same insecurities about themselves? *Will the coach validate my opinions since I'm only a second-year teacher? Will the coach label me as old school, and set in my ways, because of my many years of experience? Will the coach think I'm an effective teacher after observing me?* During the initial meeting between a coach and a teacher, the coach should first break the ice by sharing his or her insecurities. This not only conquers the fears of embarrassment and inferiority but also disarms the teacher so he or she can feel more comfortable in sharing insecurities. Teachers will appreciate the coach's human imperfections, which will allow them to start building the trust needed to cultivate relationships.

## Identification of Transparency Levels

When faced with tough opposition in the midst of change, coaches tend to become defensive and guarded, but placing a guard between the coach and the teacher is counterproductive and hinders any kind of change effort. Teachers will, however, listen to their leaders and coaches when they perceive them as co-learners alongside them on the journey of change. When coaches open up about their own failures and transparently express their motives, teachers will have a willingness to do the same. So how do we actively change the reality of what we have always done and transform the established school culture to one of transparent change? We must first address how to capture current levels of transparency in a school building.

Coaches can easily feel their way around the building, gauging transparency from personal interactions, observations of the staff's gregariousness, or perceptions of morale in faculty meetings. However, these observations may represent the perspectives of a few but in no way act as an accurate gauge of comprehensive transparency levels. Conducting a formal survey provides a better option for gauging the transparency levels throughout the building. The survey in figure 2.1 is intended to capture information from the teacher's point of view, both from a communicator and receiver perspective. The survey statements appear in pairs to measure the flow of information from teacher to leadership and leadership to teacher. Because the coach is a school leader, who does not operate in isolation from school administrators, the survey's language uses *school leadership*. Conducting the survey anonymously ensures the highest level of validity and confidence in the analysis of survey data.

Next, coaches will score and assess the survey data. Take the first paired question set, for instance.

**1a.** I have the freedom to express my own ideas to school leadership.

**1b.** School leadership freely expresses its ideas to me.

An effective survey-scoring approach to gauge transparency is to calculate the average rating for each question. Let's suppose the average teacher score for 1a was 5 (*strongly agree*) and the average teacher rating for 1b was 4 (*agree*). This gives us two pieces of useful information that I've labeled *directional transparency* and *cultural transparency*. *Directional transparency* refers to teachers' perception of their level of transparency in expressing ideas to their leaders, and

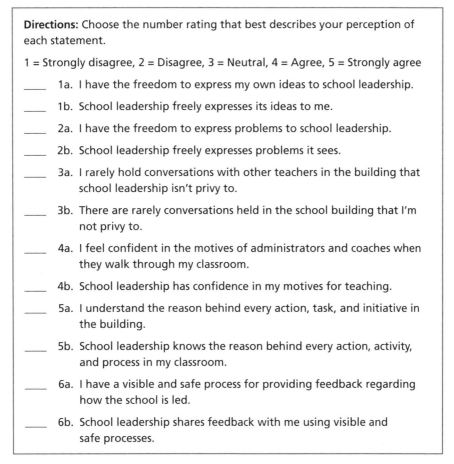

**Directions:** Choose the number rating that best describes your perception of each statement.

1 = Strongly disagree, 2 = Disagree, 3 = Neutral, 4 = Agree, 5 = Strongly agree

\_\_\_\_    1a. I have the freedom to express my own ideas to school leadership.

\_\_\_\_    1b. School leadership freely expresses its ideas to me.

\_\_\_\_    2a. I have the freedom to express problems to school leadership.

\_\_\_\_    2b. School leadership freely expresses problems it sees.

\_\_\_\_    3a. I rarely hold conversations with other teachers in the building that school leadership isn't privy to.

\_\_\_\_    3b. There are rarely conversations held in the school building that I'm not privy to.

\_\_\_\_    4a. I feel confident in the motives of administrators and coaches when they walk through my classroom.

\_\_\_\_    4b. School leadership has confidence in my motives for teaching.

\_\_\_\_    5a. I understand the reason behind every action, task, and initiative in the building.

\_\_\_\_    5b. School leadership knows the reason behind every action, activity, and process in my classroom.

\_\_\_\_    6a. I have a visible and safe process for providing feedback regarding how the school is led.

\_\_\_\_    6b. School leadership shares feedback with me using visible and safe processes.

**Figure 2.1: Teacher survey for gauging transparency.**

*Visit* **go.SolutionTree.com/instruction** *for a free reproducible version of this figure.*

their perception of leaders' level of transparency with teachers, with possibly a higher level of reservation from the leaders. *Cultural transparency* refers to the gap between the two ratings, 5 and 4, which average out to a rating of 4.5. At a comprehensive, cultural level, the freedom of expressing ideas exists throughout the building in this particular scenario. If the average were 2.5, we would conclude that neither leaders nor teachers encourage the expression of new ideas. The same analysis approach can apply to each question pair in the survey. It's fair to note that typically, the paired responses would have similar values (for example, if leadership doesn't have transparency, teachers typically don't have transparency, and vice versa). Because each school has unique circumstances, it's feasible that pockets of transparency may exist within a department but not across the building as a whole. Therefore, it's useful to evaluate both the individual values and the averaged pair values.

## Strategies for Developing Greater Transparency

Once a school has compelling data regarding transparency in the building, the school can take steps to address its communication barriers. Coaches play a pivotal role in leading the effort to establish a transparent culture. Three specific activities will help erode secretive and unhealthy communication while promoting honest and transparent ways of working: (1) walkthroughs, (2) 360-degree appraisals, and (3) weekly pulse checks.

### Walkthroughs

Coaches typically engage in walkthroughs as part of an agreed-on partnership or coaching cycle or as part of a daily process the coach or principal has previously communicated. Walkthroughs typically involve a brief appearance in the classroom for the purpose of taking the pulse of instructional effectiveness or to capture evidence or lack of evidence of learning. Too often, no subsequent feedback or affirmation occurs after short walkthroughs in the classroom, or coaches offer only minimal feedback. A coach may base the minimal feedback on something positive he or she witnessed, such as, "Your students were highly engaged in the task!" However, if a coach gave *constructive* feedback, it might sound like, "I wasn't sure of the lesson objective, nor did I see it posted." Constructive, transparent feedback should be an inherent part of the observation process.

To ensure a walkthrough gains transparent feedback, teachers and coaches must have an agreed-on standard or basis for the walkthrough. When a coach and a teacher co-develop student success outcomes and classroom *look-fors* (predetermined pieces of evidence that align with instructional goals), they form a mutual agreement on the kinds of evidence the coach will collect. A collaborative digital document (such as a Google Doc or a note in Microsoft OneNote) provides a great way to communicate and track walkthrough data. The coach co-creates this living document with the teacher, and each time the coach engages with the classroom, he or she addresses a simple checklist, a narrative, or another agreed-on indicator. The teacher doesn't have to wait for a feedback email that comes late at night or the next day; the coach's feedback updates immediately in the document.

### 360-Degree Appraisals

According to Susan Heathfield (2016), employers rely on 360-degree appraisals (or 360s) as a useful feedback tool for collecting data from peers, reporting staff members, coworkers, and customers, hence the name *360-degree appraisal*. These appraisals aid them in identifying how well employees are performing and how the employees might need to change their behaviors to create a more productive workplace. For the purposes of a coach and a teacher, it's important for the teacher to have the opportunity to provide feedback to the coach in an appraisal, rather than having a one-way dynamic where only the teacher receives input on his or her performance.

As a school leader, I admit I found it difficult to review the comments from teachers' 360s. Yes, the 360s always included positive comments, which I appreciated, but it's easy to fixate on the less-positive feedback. In hindsight, I should have requested 360s more often, even though it sometimes pained me to receive constructive comments, because those comments played an essential part in my growth as a leader. As coaches, we know that we can grow as professionals and help our teachers and students grow only when we unearth and illuminate our challenges, failures, and inefficiencies. And when I say *illuminate*, I mean share the anonymous evaluative feedback we receive with everyone. The most meaningful way to share these data is to share copies of the comments in person in a faculty meeting. This sends a clear message to the faculty: I'm willing to share my shortcomings for the sake of our growth.

## Weekly Pulse Checks

Coaches and school leaders should proactively maintain their awareness of teachers' perceptions of the school environment (for example, whether they feel the school embraces diversity and equality; whether they find the school environment conducive to positivity, creativity, innovation, and collaboration). They can share a very brief digital survey on a weekly basis, asking teachers to rate the following five items on a five-point Likert scale (where 1 means *strongly disagree* and 5 means *strongly agree*) and giving teachers an opportunity to share suggestions and wishes. Coaches and school leaders will find using this scale beneficial as they analyze the data.

1. Everyone in the building is included in communication and collaboration.
2. Your coach supports you in promoting creativity and innovation.
3. Your coach supports you in promoting positivity and passion.
4. Your coach supports you in ensuring your students' needs are met.
5. Your coach empowers you with freedom and autonomy.

Coaches will also find it effective to create open-ended questions such as the following to gauge specific feedback from teachers.

- At times, do you feel you lack the freedom to express ideas or concerns with me? If so, what verbal or nonverbal cues communicate this lack of freedom?

- What are one or two specific actions I can take to build better trust and transparency?

Coaches should share the survey scores with the entire staff and use them to not only take a pulse of the school culture but also continuously track scores for the sake of growth. Many faculty members may feel a strong personal connection to their responses, so it's important to create a comfortable setting for sharing these data. If sharing the data in a face-to-face setting, you must create a casual and friendly environment; host an informal party, open up with an icebreaker or a funny video, and so on. If you don't set this gregarious tone, an uncomfortable silence could wash over the room, which can dramatically influence the outcomes of the meeting. Sharing feedback transparently is important, but having respect for everyone's well-being is even more important.

## Conclusion

Teachers have not traditionally been given a voice to express concerns or share problems with a school leader. In toxic school cultures, leaders have even labeled teachers who share their concerns as *troublemakers* or *pot stirrers*. But a transparent culture of respect frequently exposes problems, and it positions coaches to function as intermediaries between problems and solutions. When coaches promote transparency through a supportive and trusting culture, teachers are willing to bring up issues. Exposing problems frequently creates opportunities for collaborative solutions. Coaches and leaders must make transparency a guiding principle and a building norm to create a healthy problem-solving culture. Modeling this kind of no-holds-barred mentality in which everything is fair game for discussion can turn a stagnant culture into a thriving one that hinges on open communication, sincere relationships, and trusted leaders.

# THREE

# INQUIRY

> Coaches can help teachers learn and grow not by telling them what to do but by asking questions and promoting inquiry.

The modern educational landscape widely accepts that students must possess the following skills to have success in our dynamically changing world: critical thinking, collaboration, creativity, and communication (commonly referred to as *21st century skills* or the *four Cs*; Partnership for 21st Century Skills, 2011). Ironically, educators continue to work hard at planning for instruction while underutilizing these crucial skills themselves. Teachers have become accustomed to accepting school- and district-level initiatives without inquiring as to their purpose or strategy for classroom integration. We encourage our students to question the motives behind a learning objective, or use questioning to illuminate a new facet of learning, but as educators, we struggle to approach new learning in this way. Schools must proactively prepare students for rapid changes in technology, society, and the workplace. As leaders, we must also proactively prepare teachers for these rapid changes and, furthermore, for innovation in the classroom. This requires continual learning and relentless inquiry.

The school environment, the classroom, and the teaching profession are all undergoing large-scale changes in how they function in the context of global education. As our circumstances change, so must our thinking, and so must the questions we ask. If coaches continually ask questions, they have a better chance of arriving at solutions that will move teaching and learning forward. Additionally, effective use of inquiry in instructional coaching changes the circumstances around educators and changes their own understanding of and attitude toward teaching and learning. They become keenly aware of their needs, goals, perceptions, and current reality through inquiry. This chapter explores a useful questioning model for spawning inquiry and also provides effective questioning techniques that coaches can apply in the instructional coaching context.

## Model for Spawning Inquiry

Warren Berger (2014), an innovation expert and author of the book *A More Beautiful Question*, explains that one of the most powerful forces for inspiring change in organizations and in our daily lives is a simple tool that we inherently have in all of us: questioning (or *inquiry*). Not only does inquiry help us illuminate problems, but through a purposeful approach to inquiry, our curiosity can help us create solutions and innovative ideas and inspire others in the process. Many educational and organizational cultures reward rote answers over challenging questions (Berger, 2014). Why do they do this? In part, they do this because of a societal system that originated during the Industrial Age that continues to pervade the 21st century, rewarding compliance and scalability (Rose, 2012). Seth Godin (2012) suggests that part of the rationale for shifting toward an industrialized system was the idea that educated kids would actually become more compliant and productive workers. Asking students to sit in straight rows and obey instructions didn't happen coincidentally, it was a deliberate investment for the economic future. In a nutshell, the plan was to trade short-term child-labor wages for longer-term productivity by giving kids a head start in doing what they're told. This plan is obviously irrelevant today as we're supporting students to become critical thinkers and problem solvers.

Berger (2014) states that by examining questioning and problem solving in a more organized way, we can challenge our traditional approaches and therefore evolve, change our tools, and adjust our questions according to the level of inquiry we pursue. To accomplish this, he proposes a simple three-part system to spawn inquiry: the Why–What If–How model. The *why* aspect of this model provides a helpful starting point because it challenges inquirers to halt their current line of thinking before proceeding. Berger (2014) explains that this helps people discern knowing something from knowing *how* they know something. The second part, the *what if*, helps inquirers understand a concept as thoroughly as possible and eventually create a very bold and innovative solution. This part asks them to take a no-holds-barred approach. Inquirers then have to test the solution in the real world, and that's where the *how* becomes crucial. When inquirers birth an out-of-the-box idea, they then must test it in the context of their daily work. Applying this model with very novel ideas can pose challenges, but through the iterative process and a copious amount of feedback, Berger

(2014) finds that these novel ideas can truly launch. To make this happen, we must be open and acknowledge our fears in the process.

Figure 3.1 illustrates a sample scenario of how a teacher and a coach use the Why–What If–How model to work through a situation and improve personalized learning practices in the classroom. The teacher and the coach cogenerate the questions.

---

**Scenario:** The classroom had moved toward personalized learning practices and had incorporated learning playlists. The teacher generated these playlists from algorithms based on student performance on diagnostic assessments and student progress on teacher-generated activities. The teacher noticed some students who continued to struggle with the independent work and just clicked through their assignments to finish. The teacher approached the coach to receive support on how to improve personalized learning practices in the classroom.

**Why:** Why am I using playlists in the classroom? Do they promote personalized learning? How many students have success during independent practice utilizing playlists? What are the positives of using playlists during independent practice? What purpose does personalized learning serve? Are there other ways of facilitating personalized learning in the classroom?

**What If:** What if we continued using playlists that use technology to create individualized pathways for each student, but incorporated other personalized learning strategies in the classroom? Playlists are just one tool to help promote learning—what if we use them in tandem with other strategies?

**How:** How can I improve personalized learning strategies in conjunction with playlists? (The teacher observes student dispositions during independent practice. If the teacher notices students clicking through their assignments just to finish or becoming unengaged, the teacher will re-engage the student or group of students by having brief conferences about how they feel about their learning progress, and the teacher will provide an alternate activity to engage students in learning while targeting individualized skills. The teacher could do this through pairs or small groups of students, through teacher-facilitated small-group instruction, or through a gamified learning experience.)

---

**Figure 3.1: Why–What If–How model example.**

This model produces effective results because it has foundations in questioning. When engaging with this model, coaches and teachers need to ensure they ask the right questions to achieve the outcomes they desire—they must choose effective questions.

# Effective Questioning

Berger (2014) explains that the most creative and successful people tend to be expert questioners. Having mastered the art of inquiry, these expert questioners raise questions no one else does and discover powerful solutions. Berger (2014) cites organizations such as Google, Netflix, IDEO, and Airbnb that embrace this type of questioning, noting that they all became successful because they incorporated a relentless focus on effective questioning. Educators may find effective questioning difficult but can simplify it by incorporating structured and explicit approaches such as the question formulation technique (QFT) and the five most important questions framework.

## Question Formulation Technique

Researchers Dan Rothstein, Luz Santana, and Andrew Minigan (2015) of the Right Question Institute (RQI) developed the QFT process (a deceptively simple process) to help teachers provide students with both structure and the opportunity to practice generating and working with their own questions. By going through the steps of the process, students learn to think divergently, convergently, and metacognitively.

Because we are all learners, coaches can similarly employ the QFT process to assist in leading change, growing professionally, and becoming deeper thinkers. Once coaches develop the skill of inquiry through the QFT process, they should facilitate this process with teachers to refine pedagogy and increase student learning. The QFT process involves the following seven steps (Right Question Institute, n.d.).

1. Identifying a question focus
2. Following the rules for producing questions
3. Producing questions
4. Improving questions
5. Prioritizing questions
6. Establishing next steps
7. Reflecting

The following sections will discuss these steps in the context of how coaches should support teachers with inquiry-based strategies to improve collaboration, planning, and classroom instruction.

### Identifying a Question Focus

The process of producing questions can challenge many people. Therefore, the initial step in the question formulation technique, created for teaching all people no matter their level of education, centers on identifying a question focus (QFocus). The QFocus functions as a starting point for question formulation. The QFocus itself is not a question. It is a clear, thought-provoking topic, problem, or situation (for example, next-generation learning spaces or whole-child education) that serves as a foundation to build questions. Coaches can facilitate a fishbowl or another idea-generating learning protocol to help flesh out topics that are thought provoking and tied to existing issues for teachers.

### Following the Rules for Producing Questions

The QFT process puts in place four rules to follow to support question formulation (Right Question Institute, n.d.):

1. Ask as many questions as you can.

2. Do not stop to discuss, judge, or answer any questions.

3. Write down every question exactly as it is stated.

4. Change any statement into a question.

Because the QFT process is unique, teachers may find it challenging to follow these rules initially. In this step, coaches need to create buy-in for rule following and discuss challenges so teachers can follow the QFT process with fidelity; then the process can yield the best results. Coaches can create buy-in by discussing the learning protocols that teachers facilitate with their students and illuminating the value of these kinds of structures to guide inquiry.

### Producing Questions

Teachers will use the QFocus from step 1 to formulate as many questions as possible in this step. Coaches should encourage teachers to ask all kinds of questions about their chosen topic, problem, or situation, while following the four rules for producing questions. This step encourages a free flow of questions (the coach records the teachers' questions and thoughts that spawn from this step) and discourages a focus on question quality (which the next step will address).

### Improving Questions

Once teachers generate a list of questions, they will sort and examine the questions for ways they can improve them by following a process that involves three steps.

1. Teachers differentiate between two types of questions
   they generated in their list: (a) closed-ended questions and

(b) open-ended questions. People can answer *closed-ended questions* with *yes* or *no* or another one-word response, and *open-ended questions* require an explanation. Teachers scan through their list of questions and mark the closed-ended questions with a *C* and the open-ended questions with an *O*.

2.  Teachers reflect on the Cs and Os and explain the advantages and disadvantages of asking each type of question. This step helps them see the value in both types of questions.

3.  Teachers change at least one question from one type to the other. The question they choose to change should be a question they feel resonates the most or one that might yield solutions most strongly related to the QFocus. Making this change will help them learn how to edit their questions to meet their purpose.

### Prioritizing Questions

After teachers have sorted and examined their list of questions, they will choose three questions they identify as priorities based on actions they want to take. For example, they might choose three questions they consider the most important, three questions they want to address first, or three questions they want to explore further. They should identify their rationale for making these questions priorities. For example, they might rationalize, "The questions I chose will better motivate me to collaborate with my colleagues because of my inexperience with this new change initiative."

### Establishing Next Steps

Now, the questions are ready for teachers to decide how to put them into action. In this step, teachers respond to the prompt, How will you use your questions? Teachers might respond, for example, that they will use their questions to conduct research or refine a lesson, or as a guide to lead to change.

### Reflecting

In the last step of the QFT process, teachers reflect on what they have learned and how they can apply new learning. Reflecting helps teachers internalize the process, its value, and how to further expand on new learning. Recording their reflections further supports fidelity to this process.

Figure 3.2 provides a tool to help facilitate the QFT process. While coaches can use this tool to support teacher inquiry, they can also benefit from applying the QFT process to reflect on their own work and attitudes. The following example illustrates how an instructional coach might use the QFT process to reflect on his or her work with teachers and his or her attitude toward change.

**Step 1: Identifying a Question Focus**

*Quote: If you always do what you've always done, you will always get what you've always got.*

**Step 2: Following the Rules for Producing Questions**

Record what you might find difficult about the following rules.

1. Ask as many questions as you can.

2. Do not stop to discuss, judge, or answer any questions.

3. Write down every question exactly as it is stated.

4. Change any statement into a question.

*I tend to judge my questions as I ask them. I tend to measure my words as I produce them.*

**Step 3: Producing Questions**

Record your questions about the QFocus.

1. *How do I discern those things I've done that are effective?*

2. *How do I find the source of ineffective practices?*

3. *Will teachers find this quote motivating?*

4. *How do I move teachers forward once they feel inspired and actually empower them to act?*

5. *How do I decide to do the things I do in my daily work?*

6. *Do I have an accurate picture of the results I get?*

7. *How can I measure results better?*

8. *Do my actions relate back to specific goals or a vision?*

9. *How do I turn my past errors and mistakes into success today?*

10. *Why do I resist change?*

**Step 4: Improving Questions**

Closed-ended questions can be answered with *yes* or *no* or another one-word response.

Open-ended questions require an explanation and cannot be answered with *yes* or *no* or another one-word response.

a. Review your list of questions, and mark the open-ended questions with an *O* and the closed-ended questions with a *C*.

1. *How do I discern those things I've done that are effective? (O)*

2. *How do I find the source of ineffective practices? (O)*

3. *Will teachers find this quote motivating? (C)*

**Figure 3.2: QFT process example.**                    continued ➜

4. *How do I move teachers forward once they feel inspired and actually empower them to act? (O)*

5. *How do I decide to do the things I do in my daily work? (O)*

6. *Do I have an accurate picture of the results I get? (C)*

7. *How can I measure results better? (O)*

8. *Do my actions relate back to specific goals or a vision? (C)*

9. *How do I turn my past errors and mistakes into success today? (O)*

10. *Why do I resist change? (O)*

b. Name the advantages and disadvantages of asking closed-ended questions.

| Advantages | Disadvantages |
|---|---|
| • *They promote clarity.*<br>• *They are quick and easy to generate.*<br>• *You use less cognitive load to answer them.*<br>• *More people have the ability to generate them.* | • *They are excessively simplistic; most complex questions can't be answered with a simple <u>yes</u> or <u>no</u>.*<br>• *They may not fully represent real-world thinking or scenarios.* |

c. Name the advantages and disadvantages of asking open-ended questions.

| Advantages | Disadvantages |
|---|---|
| • *They allow you to develop multiple answers and solutions.*<br>• *They promote critical and divergent thinking and creativity.*<br>• *They can help spawn more complex questions that get to the crux of a matter.* | • *They take longer to generate.*<br>• *Variance in solutions could create ambiguity.* |

d. Change one closed-ended question into an open-ended question, and change one open-ended question into a closed-ended one.

• *Do my actions relate back to specific goals or a vision? (C) changes to (O) What actions do I take that relate back to the school vision, and how do I know this is the case?*

• *How do I find the source of ineffective practices? (O) changes to (C) Can I change any ineffective practices right now?*

**Step 5: Prioritizing Questions**

a. Choose the three most important questions from your list. Mark them with an *X*.

   *X  How do I discern those things I've done that are effective?*

   *X  How do I turn my past errors and mistakes into success today?*

   *X  Why do I resist change?*

b. Record the reasons you selected these three.

   *The questions I've chosen represent questions that will most challenge my thinking, push me to innovative solutions, and lead me to create actionable goals.*

c. Record the numbers of your priority questions.

   *1, 9, and 10.*

**Step 6: Establishing Next Steps**

How will you use your questions?

*I will use these questions to create an action plan to transform teaching and learning in my school. These questions illuminate the preconceptions I have regarding learning, pedagogy, leadership, and instructional practices in my school. They will assist me in identifying the failures and setbacks in my work as a coach, and in leveraging those experiences for positive change. The questions will spawn actionable steps that make my work as a coach more effective.*

**Step 7: Reflecting**

a. What did you learn? Record your reflections.

   *I learned that many of the activities and tasks I busy myself with on a daily basis don't have strong roots in the <u>why</u> of our work as educators. Typically, the urgent tasks have loose connections to grandiose goals and get in the way of truly important work. I also learned through this metacognition that I resist change in my life too, and as a result, I have become more empathetic in my approach to change.*

b. What is the value of what you learned? Record your reflections.

   *The quote used for the QFocus often gets overstated and has lost its meaning over time. Most educators would agree with this statement, but they often let it reside as an inspirational statement, instead of using it to move to empowerment and action. This QFT activity helped me go beyond using the phrase to create actionable steps to help others improve teaching and learning.*

*Source: Adapted from Right Question Institute, n.d.*

*Visit go.SolutionTree.com/instruction for a free reproducible version of this figure.*

Coaches can similarly use this tool to facilitate teacher reflection on any issues that could benefit from further inquiry. Managing change will remain a fundamental and continual process as we, as coaches, all grow in our profession.

Using the QFT process can give coaches perspective on the attitudes and beliefs teachers hold about a specific topic. Coaches may find this process particularly useful at the beginning of a new change initiative or as a solution builder to an emerging issue. Additionally, the QFT process works to develop teachers' questioning and inquiry-building skills.

## Five Most Important Questions Framework

Another fascinating resource that helps organizations ask crucial questions to uncover problems and develop innovative solutions is Peter Drucker's (2008) book *The Five Most Important Questions You Will Ever Ask About Your Organization*. Drucker (2008) solidly builds the framework of his writing on five essential questions.

1. What is our mission?

2. Who is our customer?

3. What does the customer value?

4. What are our results?

5. What is our plan?

Given the language Drucker (2008) uses, this framework undoubtedly has origins in business acumen. But you can apply it to leadership, education, and coaching in a very powerful way if you use the term *customer* to refer to the *who* you directly serve: students, teachers, and administrators. The customer often changes depending on the specific mission. If the mission involves learning strategies, your customers would primarily be students. If it involves changing the culture of teaching in the building, that would make teachers the customers. When you reflect on what the customer values, keep in mind that values do not remain static. Depending on building initiatives or district strategic work, values can change with new circumstances, new leadership, new teachers, and new students. Figure 3.3 provides an example of how an instructional coach could adapt Drucker's (2008) five-question framework to support teacher inquiry. By reflecting on our work through these questions, we can clearly identify why we do what we do as coaches, how to improve our work, and how to develop a purposeful plan with specific actions to help us achieve our goals.

To create demand for inquiry, coaches can help teachers identify their goals or learning objectives—for example, preparing students for a dynamically changing world of innovation and problem solving. As coaches, we must also

**1. What is your mission?**

*My mission is to support teachers as they develop instruction that aligns with our new personalized learning focus for the school. We have discussed personalized learning at the surface level, but we have been empowered to go deeper with the concept by developing a plan that will ensure every student receives differentiated, targeted, and personalized support.*

**2. Who is your customer?**

*My primary customers will be teachers, as I will collaborate with each grade level to create aligned goals and will stay highly engaged in co-teaching and co-planning. Additionally, I will work with administrators to ensure fidelity of implementation of personalized learning. I will also work with students to measure student engagement and motivation throughout the process.*

**3. What does your customer value?**

*The teachers I work alongside value guidance, support, trust, and resourcefulness. As I organize my tasks for the day, what my teachers value will be the primary determining factor in how I approach my work. They would like encouragement, modeling, an extra set of eyes and ears, feedback, and a thought partner.*

**4. What results do you seek?**

*I (along with all stakeholders) aim to increase student learning through self-direction and customization. To drive this vision, teachers will embrace multiple approaches to help students determine the pace of learning, create opportunities to use various technology tools, differentiate content according to needs, and create flexible environments that promote creativity and critical thinking.*

**5. What is your plan?**

*In collaboration with administrators and teachers, I will facilitate the development of a schoolwide personalized learning plan that will incorporate innovative solutions to promote more independent learning, flexible and collaborative classroom environments, strategic and focused use of edtech tools, and purposeful small-group instruction. I will use our district SMART goal template to create agreed-on goals that are measurable and that we can re-evaluate and revise.*

**Figure 3.3: Five-question framework example.**

partner with teachers as change agents and inquirers to further ensure we create classrooms that cultivate innovation. The examples in the figures throughout this chapter create a context for coaches to apply the QFT process and the five-question framework to their daily work both in individual reflections and in a collaborative environment. These inquiry-based resources should be used in both individual reflections and in a collaborative environment to provide the most in-depth exploration of the current reality and high-quality question outcomes.

# Conclusion

We can best explore how instructional coaching relates to and can enhance learning by asking questions. The inquiry process promotes self-direction for any learner (teacher, coach, or student) as the learner readily creates and revises his or her own questions and dives into concepts that truly have relevance to his or her work. For coaches, these concepts may include: How does coaching affect those it touches? How does it cause us to see the classroom differently? How does it change the cycle of thinking and learning? How does it connect concepts, experiences, actions, and behaviors? and How can we use it to produce struggle in learning that deepens our thinking? For teachers, these concepts may include: How does instruction affect my students' thinking and learning in meaningful ways? How does my role cause students to see the classroom differently? and How does the struggle in the teaching profession deepen my own thinking about instruction and learning? I encourage you to reflect on these questions not only as you read this book but as you determine your current mission, your *why*, your *what if*, and your *how* and what the teachers in your building value. Phenomenal educators value inquiry. Learners yearn for inquiry. The more we question through instructional coaching, the closer we come to grasping the true essence of teaching and learning.

# FOUR

# DISCOURSE

> Coaches can purposefully use language in a way that creates a discourse to convey to a teacher that they value him or her as a person and a professional and value his or her ideas.

Because our students' future is at stake, coaching must increasingly focus on continuous improvement, student achievement, learning gaps, teacher efficacy, and change leadership. Leaders may claim they focus on these points, but upon gauging their everyday language and discourse, there's often misalignment between what coaches, as leaders, mean and what they say. For example, a school or district mission statement may emphasize a nurturing culture to support rigorous thinking and meaningful learning experiences, but the principal and coach frequently emphasize that teachers must follow a static and prescriptive curricular program. The coach's language sets the tone and foundation for every interaction that follows it. It is important that a coach's tone in interactions with teachers facilitates positive relationships that empower teachers to succeed. In a relational culture of trust and transparency, and with previous positive experiences, the coach can effectively use empowering discourse.

While Graham Nuthall (n.d.) notes that "*discourse* refers to the language that teachers and students use to communicate with each other in the classroom," for the purposes of this book's focus on the coach-teacher relationship, this chapter will refer to *discourse* as the language used among all learners in the school building, specifically between the coach and the teacher. This chapter will examine strategies to help coaches create a culture of healthy and effective discourse and will then explore how to identify the existing culture of discourse to determine which strategies to employ to improve the culture.

## Strategies for Creating a Culture of Healthy and Effective Discourse

Coaches should create and support a culture of effective communication and discourse in their building. They do this by using strategies that include speaking tentatively, reconceptualizing problems, communicating with purpose, and fostering intrinsic motivation. The following sections will unpack these strategies.

### Speaking Tentatively

Initially, *speaking tentatively* may sound like a counterintuitive approach to coaching and may even make the coach appear ineffective or not credible. This is understandable, given that past trends and traditional (postindustrial) leadership lend credence to the traits of assertiveness and dominance giving power and influence to communication (Grant, 2014). Adam Grant (2014) counters this traditional thinking through his principles of tentative speech or, as he refers to it, *powerless communication*. Powerless communicators speak in ways that display vulnerability through their use of hesitations and disclaimers. Grant (2014) explains how powerless communication builds influence because those who use it ask questions instead of giving answers, speak tentatively instead of with assertion, and ask for advice over declaring their expert opinions. Grant (2014) refers to powerless-speech signals used in conversations that communicate a willingness to defer to the other person or to take others' opinions into consideration. When you, as the coach, use tentative-speech signals, stakeholders lower their resistance because they don't feel as if you're trying to convince or trick them. Powerless speakers communicate they are receptive to suggestions and open to advice.

When communicating with teachers, coaches should not only be aware but proactive in establishing language norms. The following list of examples, based on Alison Fragale's (2006) research on what she calls *powerless speech*, can help guide coaches in establishing norms that exemplify tentative language. In situations where people are expected to collaborate in a group setting, speech that contains these "powerless" elements has a much greater effect in gaining respect.

Before exploring these examples, it's essential to address that some readers may initially feel that these communication methods may come off as disingenuous. However, the focus is not on trying to avoid being direct or honest, but on lowering resistance to the message. The aim is for coaches to display humility by making conscious decisions about their tone and demeanor. Additionally, readers may have a concern that this language may call into question their professional capabilities or intelligence. It is important to understand that using tentative language should not make a coach seem less intelligent, but rather allow the teacher to have every opportunity to be empowered to act. Examples of powerless speech include the following.

- **Hesitations:** "Well," "um," and "you know"
- **Hedges:** "Kinda," "sorta," "maybe," and "probably"
- **Disclaimers:** "This may be a bad idea but . . ."
- **Tag questions:** "That's interesting, isn't it?" and "That's a good idea, right?"
- **Intensifiers:** "Really," "very," and "quite"

Suppose you were developing a personalized professional development framework for teachers and you wanted to get input from leadership teams across the school. During a meeting, you share the new vision for professional learning, but you want to ensure that discourse incorporates powerless speech to keep the conversation open and empowering. The following list adapts the powerless-communication elements to provide sample statements that you could integrate into discourse.

- **Hesitations:** "You know, education and our classrooms have changed significantly. It's time for our professional development to follow suit."
- **Hedges:** "We are sorta surprised by how much value teachers find in informal professional development like Twitter chats. We would kinda like to incorporate this in our plan."
- **Disclaimers:** "This may be a bad idea, but we won't know if this technology tool will make a difference until we implement it effectively and give it time."
- **Tag questions:** "While we focus on providing students with easy access to curriculum and learning, we don't really focus on this for teachers. That's interesting, isn't it?"
- **Intensifiers:** "This personalized learning plan is very bold and represents a line of thinking we haven't explored before."

Note that we use powerless speech to build respect, influence, and trust with teachers so we can disarm any strong initial responses that might result from aversion to change. Additionally, this discourse is meant to empower teacher voice in the decision-making process. It's important that we have a clear vision but condone speaking tentatively about how we will accomplish this new vision.

## Reconceptualizing Problems

As coaches, we focus much of our work on solving problems, from helping a teacher think through the most effective small-group instruction to helping create a schoolwide professional development plan. Problem solving takes perseverance, patience, and the skill of working with diverse personalities. Problem solving is a bittersweet paradox of frustration, stress, and mentally and emotionally draining work paired with the thrill of excitement, inspiration, courage, and satisfaction that comes with success.

Oftentimes, coaches believe they support teachers by removing barriers and obstacles (and even attempting to do so) for their teammates. I once witnessed a coach create common formative assessments for teachers because the teachers had limited time to do so themselves. Creating common formative assessments for teachers doesn't deliver a long-term solution for helping teachers manage time effectively, and furthermore, the "doing the work for you" mentality erodes the coach-teacher relationship. A culture of effective discourse must include dialogue that does not center solely on removing barriers and that reconceptualizes problems as collaborative learning opportunities.

Like the butterfly that must struggle within a chrysalis to gain strength and grow its wings, struggle is necessary to strengthen our practice. Struggle can produce growth if leveraged in a way that effectively utilizes problem solving and reflection. Instead of creating common formative assessments for teachers, the coach can create discourse that will reconceptualize problem solving from an easy (but ineffective) perceived quick fix to a more purposeful and sustainable (effective) opportunistic approach. Communication from the coach would sound like this:

> *Thank you for all the hard work and time you put into the important task of creating assessments to inform your instruction. It would save you time for me to create common formative assessments for the team, but it would do a disservice to you, as my role as a coach is to provide instructional support. I am reworking our scheduled meeting time to create a more focused and structured time for our team to collaboratively create common formative assessments. Once we establish roles and new protocols for deconstructing content standards, creating assessment items, and evaluating student responses using appropriate technology tools, we will not only have the ability to create consistency across our team but will also have more effective planning, instruction, and feedback processes. The more consistent and purposeful our collaborative assessment meetings become, the more efficiency we will have in our daily work.*

Notice the communication acknowledges the teachers' hard work and the problem (not enough time to create common formative assessments). The discourse highlights that its purpose is not to remove the problem but to address the problem in an opportunistic way that allows the coach and teachers to solve the problem creatively and innovatively, with the goal of becoming better teachers for their students.

Instead of communicating their desire to minimize problems for teachers, coaches should focus their communication (and, more important, their actions) on leveraging problems to create opportunities for growth. Their discourse should center on transforming problems into exciting and unique opportunities to create, learn, and innovate together.

## Communicating With Purpose

Purposeful communication ties back to the mission of the school community and the vision shared by all those in the school building. It inspires grandiose dreams and spawns meaningful work. Before we address what communicating with purpose looks like, we must differentiate between purpose and another often-associated word: *passion*. *Passionate* is an adjective that receives a good amount of hype. Every coach desires to work with a passionate, positive teacher, as does every student. As educators Starr Sackstein and Nathan Lang (2016) explain, "People are naturally attracted to positive energy. It affirms an inner joy and creates a pleasant emotion." It's especially coveted inside an environment of apathy, or in a culture of stagnancy (Hudgens, 2016).

However, passion can often be circumstantial and based on what excites someone at a particular point in his or her life. Parts of life and work may be dull and difficult necessities that require self-discipline for us to deal with them. These things require us to have a strong purpose, so we can endure them to achieve something larger. If we had a choice, we would rather focus on, dream about, and spend time doing something we feel passionate about. Passion can inspire, but alone, it will not create action.

Passion isn't the enemy, and it certainly creates motivation for students. Sackstein (2016) explains how passion projects create deep learning and engagement for students and have created helpful ways for teachers to get to know their students' interests. Passion has a place in the classroom, especially for invoking student interest and motivation. Passion also has a place in the daily work of a teacher, as he or she relies on those sparks of energy to create new ideas, innovate, and initiate change. However, a driving force stronger than passion is *purpose*.

In his book *Ego Is the Enemy*, Ryan Holiday (2016) explains that *passion* is *about* something (for example, "I am so passionate *about* _____"), while *purpose* is *to* and *for* something (for example, "I must do _____ in order *to* _____," "I am wired to accomplish _____ in order *to* _____," or "I must struggle through _____ *for* the sake of _____"). Notice that purpose de-emphasizes the *I*. Purpose is about pursuing something outside oneself, as opposed to pursuing something to benefit oneself. Purpose is about giving time, resources, and energy to a vision bigger than oneself. What does this comparison of the two terms mean in the context of the coach-teacher discourse? Consider the juxtaposition of a coach's passion and purpose statements in table 4.1.

**Table 4.1: Passion Versus Purpose**

| Statements of Passion | Statements of Purpose |
|---|---|
| "I am so excited about sharing this new instructional strategy I just learned with you." | "I am willing to spend the necessary time with you to learn alongside you so we can help students grow and thrive." |
| "I am so excited to make your classroom the exemplar because it really makes our school look good." | "We must use your classroom as the exemplar because of the learning and growth opportunities we can create for our teacher teams." |

Passion tends to focus on *me*, and purpose relates to something bigger than *me*. When one faces difficult challenges, passion can wane, whereas purpose becomes stronger (Sackstein & Lang, 2016). Passion gives you the *motivation* to coach or to teach, but purpose is *why* you coach or teach. Communicating with purpose provides direction for all stakeholders. The following list shares specific suggestions for ways coaches can support discourse by communicating with purpose (Sackstein & Lang, 2016).

- Coaches share about the things that make them uncomfortable and the times they have conquered fear to do something because of their purpose in education or instructional coaching.

- Action-driven coaches communicate the value they place on the hard work a team displays to reach a lofty goal. Some of the team's work happens behind the scenes and, therefore, the coach should illuminate this work to create a sense of synergy. This "hidden" work should be exposed as much as possible during team meetings, faculty meetings, informal conversations, and so on.

- Coaches ask fellow educators (principals, instructional coaches, teachers, and so on) to become mentors (or communicate a desired co-learning relationship that they do not specifically have to label with a *mentor-mentee* designation). These mentors have a compelling vision for how to reach all students and have proven themselves successful. They have proven their walk matches their talk.

- Coaches speak with ease, sincerity, and no hidden agenda. They honestly communicate their own thoughts about new or re-emerging ideas. They seek feedback from trusted peers, examine areas of individual growth, and become more malleable each day as they encounter new facts and evidence. Coaches feel comfortable in their own skin, have confidence in themselves, and honor their past experiences and journeys.

- Coaches are humbled and don't believe they are the smartest or the most experienced people in the room. They look outside themselves for new ways to improve teaching and learning. To gain new perspectives and knowledge, coaches surround themselves with people who are different from them and who think differently than they do.

Communicating with purpose also means that we recognize and affirm teachers in a meaningful, frequent, and consistent way for actions that have real value. According to Dweck (2007), what people think about their own intelligence has a marked influence on their motivation to learn. A *growth mindset* exists when people believe they can develop their intelligence. Those with a *fixed mindset* think of intelligence as being a fixed quality that one either has or does not have. Dweck (2007) concludes that when educators praise students for their intellectual ability, it doesn't increase motivation and resilience but instead encourages a fixed mindset. In contrast, praising students for the effort they put forth and how they process learning (through engagement, perseverance, strategy, improvement, and the like) promotes sustainable motivation. It tells students what they've done to succeed and what they need to do to succeed again in the future. We can apply Dweck's (2007) extensive growth mindset work to adult learners—both teachers and coaches—who have a desire to continually learn, grow, and experience personal and professional success. Coaches should learn new skills and acquire new knowledge alongside teachers. Coaches should highlight their own failures as they happen, and focus on how they learned from those experiences in the process of seeking a growth mindset.

## Fostering Intrinsic Motivation

Maybe you have been in a classroom where you've heard a teacher use this kind of communication with a student: "If you do _____, then you'll get _____." (For example, "If you complete your reading log, you'll get a better grade.") These carrot-and-stick-driven teacher-centric statements come from a place of compliance, with no connection to the student's motivation or identity. This same scenario unfolds in adult discourse in the building: "If you turn in your lesson plans on time, you won't get a nagging email from the principal. If your students receive high test scores, you'll receive a positive evaluation." While high expectations play an integral part in any classroom or school culture, we should not ground our communication of these expectations in compliance.

What if coaches shift their communication focus from conveying high expectations to inspiring aspirations? Dweck (2007) explains that students have more intrinsic motivation if they feel inspired to act in a way that exemplifies their identity as they learn and gain achievements. The same conclusion applies to teachers as reflective learners. Effective praise should communicate that the actions themselves (and the person doing them) contribute to the greater good and not necessarily because they appease the person providing the praise. Table 4.2 provides a few examples of how coaches (communicators) can begin to change their daily language with teachers (receivers) to make this shift in focus. The left side of the table includes communicator-centric expectations that have their basis in compliance. The right side provides examples of how to transform the expectations to exemplify more aspirationally motivated communication that focuses on the receiver.

Notice that the aspirational statements on the right are not as direct as the statements on the left but instead serve as prompts. Using aspirations, instead of directives, in our coaching discourse to frame the desired action motivates teachers to act out of desire and purpose.

Coaches can make their discourse very effective if they purposefully and positively keep it focused on teachers' aspirations and if they clearly connect teachers' actions (work ethic, collaboration, perseverance, and so on) to the resulting professional outcomes (effects, performance, growth goals, and so on). Coaches must provide teachers with the recognition, affirmation, praise, and feedback they not only deserve but also need.

**Table 4.2: Transforming Expectations to Aspirations**

| Communicator-Centric Expectations | Receiver-Centric Aspirations |
|---|---|
| "I need you all to close your laptops during the meeting." | "How can we all get the most out of today's meeting?" |
| "I need your lesson plan before we have our preconference." | "Do you have everything you need to prepare for our preconference together?" |
| "Next time, make sure you state the learning objective at the beginning of the lesson." | "Did students understand why they were doing the activity? Is it important that they understand this? How do we ensure that happens?" |
| "I'm not seeing growth. I think it might suit you better to teach at another grade level or in another content area." | "We are a team, and I'm in this with you for the long haul. How do you feel about current challenges and struggles?" |
| "Reflect after the lesson so we can have a productive debrief." | "I will record my reflection right after the lesson so I can accurately capture everything surrounding the goals we've created together. I'm looking forward to hearing your reflection on the lesson!" |

# Assessment of Existing Culture

Before we, as coaches, can make decisions and develop strategies to cultivate effective discourse, we must determine the existing language norms in the building. The school most likely has not previously established agreed-on language norms, but it has unspoken norms that reflect the culture in the building. Figure 4.1 (page 46) provides a useful audit tool to gauge the level at which adults in the school environment speak tentatively (items 1–4), reconceptualize problems (items 5–8), and communicate with purpose (items 9–12). Not only should the coach and school leadership complete this audit, but teachers or teams of teachers should participate as well. Ask each individual or team to rate each item using a Likert scale of 1 to 5 (where 1 means *strongly disagree* and 5 means *strongly agree*). Coaches should note any statement that receives a rating of 3 or less and discuss it further, either in a small group or in a one-on-one setting.

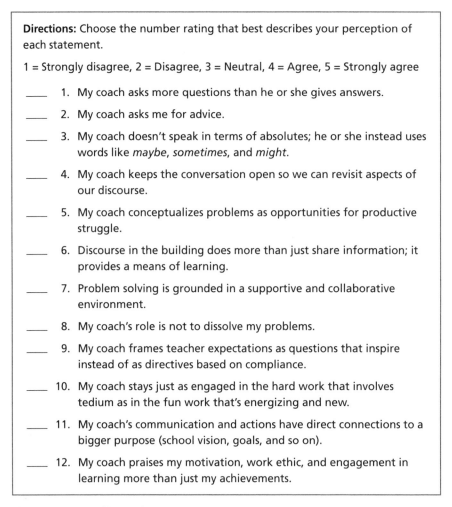

**Directions:** Choose the number rating that best describes your perception of each statement.

1 = Strongly disagree, 2 = Disagree, 3 = Neutral, 4 = Agree, 5 = Strongly agree

\_\_\_\_  1.  My coach asks more questions than he or she gives answers.

\_\_\_\_  2.  My coach asks me for advice.

\_\_\_\_  3.  My coach doesn't speak in terms of absolutes; he or she instead uses words like *maybe*, *sometimes*, and *might*.

\_\_\_\_  4.  My coach keeps the conversation open so we can revisit aspects of our discourse.

\_\_\_\_  5.  My coach conceptualizes problems as opportunities for productive struggle.

\_\_\_\_  6.  Discourse in the building does more than just share information; it provides a means of learning.

\_\_\_\_  7.  Problem solving is grounded in a supportive and collaborative environment.

\_\_\_\_  8.  My coach's role is not to dissolve my problems.

\_\_\_\_  9.  My coach frames teacher expectations as questions that inspire instead of as directives based on compliance.

\_\_\_\_  10.  My coach stays just as engaged in the hard work that involves tedium as in the fun work that's energizing and new.

\_\_\_\_  11.  My coach's communication and actions have direct connections to a bigger purpose (school vision, goals, and so on).

\_\_\_\_  12.  My coach praises my motivation, work ethic, and engagement in learning more than just my achievements.

**Figure 4.1: Audit tool.**

*Visit **go.SolutionTree.com/instruction** for a free reproducible version of this figure.*

The score ratings will help define aspects of discourse (speaking tentatively, reconceptualizing problems, and communicating with purpose) that the coach and school leadership need to address. Discussing and determining why certain items receive high or low ratings will also help the coach and school leaders determine what changes to make.

For aspects on the audit that receive an average rating that is lower than 3, the coach and school leaders can consider the following three guiding questions.

1.  How can I incorporate strategies from this chapter to move speech from assertive to tentative?

2.  How can I incorporate strategies in this chapter to reconceptualize problems in a way that promotes better solutions and a healthier culture?

3. How can I incorporate strategies from this chapter to change my communication approach from reactive to purposeful?

Reflecting on the strategies noted in these questions will help coaches and school leaders identify solutions and ways to improve their discourse.

## Conclusion

Dialogue that takes place in an environment of compliance can often support a fear-based system of rules in which teachers pretend to be people they're not in order to avoid rejection or marginalization. An unhealthy environment of dialogue encourages teachers to mimic the actions that they believe the coach or school leader finds favorable. In a sense, they copy the perceived beliefs of the most influential person in the school building. This results in teachers saying what they think the coach wants to hear, rather than participating in a productive discourse.

When we have a highly relational, multidirectional, clear, continual, and growth-centered discourse, we cultivate a transformational culture that leads to genuine and sustainable coach-teacher relationships. Reconceptualizing problems creates opportunities to communicate that we value teachers and care about their challenges to the extent that we, as coaches, are willing to put in the time and support to learn and help create solutions alongside the teachers.

Sackstein and Lang (2016) explain, "Purpose is the foundation of a compelling vision . . . a vision far greater than our self-centered passion." Communicating with purpose creates an environment of discourse that focuses on our motivation to do the hard work. By intrinsically motivating teachers, coaches can accomplish compelling work without the ineffective efforts of directives or compliance. Empowering language is contagious and becomes the cultural norm when we embed it deeply in purposeful discourse.

# FIVE

# REVERBERATION

> Reverberation allows coaches to create meaningful feedback and metafeedback processes characterized by consistent dialogue that fosters trusting relationships.

In an era of teacher-performance evaluations tied to specific building or district initiatives, teacher self-efficacy often hinges on moving targets and is subject to fluctuations caused by a changing school focus. Just as teachers have a desire to empower students to take ownership of their learning, coaches desire to provide feedback that empowers teachers to make decisions that will result in progress toward their individual or team goals.

*Feedback* is not a new term, but it has certainly become a buzzword in education. Simply, John Hattie and Gregory Yates (2014) define *feedback* as information that supports the learner in reducing the gap between where the learner currently is and where the learner could go. According to John Hattie and Helen Timperley (2007), "Feedback is one of the most powerful influences on learning and achievement, but this impact can be either positive or negative" (p. 81). The person receiving the feedback on areas to improve can interpret it negatively as "I did something wrong" or "I'm not very good." He or she may also interpret it positively as "This aspect is something the coach can help me improve on" or "This gives us an opportunity to learn and grow together." This chapter will examine practices that help frame feedback positively for both the coach and the teacher.

Coaches have introduced *feedback loops* (previously utilized in the corporate world) in teacher teams as a means of professional growth and evaluation. A feedback loop is a style of back-and-forth dialogue to ensure feedback continually improves behavior or solves a problem. Researchers Edwin A. Locke, Norman Cartledge, and Claramae S. Knerr (1970) first introduced leveraging feedback loops for effective goal setting. They found that when people receive meaningful feedback regarding their performance relative to goals that have been assigned to them, they will use the feedback to evaluate and adjust their actions to better achieve the goals. Additionally, psychologist Albert Bandura (1977) coined the term *self-efficacy*, referring to one's belief in his or her own ability to succeed on the journey toward his or her goals. Effective feedback loops build positive momentum and self-efficacy and therefore positively impact behavior because they promote increased communication between the coach and teacher.

Building on feedback loops, I propose what I call a *reverberation cycle*. Feedback loops generally refer to the process of endless feedback, moving past the "one and done" style of feedback, but don't specify the communicative nature between the communicator and receiver. *Reverberation* is the persistence of sound after it's been produced. For feedback to transform teaching and learning, feedback must continually remain a thread in the fabric of coaching—hence the name *reverberation cycle*. The reverberation cycle comprises a two-way oscillation of feedback, from teacher to coach and coach to teacher. It's a cycle because it never ends, and the oscillating feedback will regress or progress around the cyclic loop, depending on individual need and circumstance.

This chapter explores the power of feedback as it relates to instructional coaching through the driver of reverberation. It will investigate a structure—the reverberation cycle—that builds on feedback loops and explain how coaches can balance constructive feedback with praise, engage in informal dialogue, and facilitate their own professional growth to support pedagogy and teacher professional learning and create a culture of reverberation.

## Reverberation Cycle

In a reverberation cycle, the coach invites teachers to give feedback not only on their own progress but also on how the coach has supported their learning and growth. The fact that this cycle is truly a two-way reverberation allows the teachers to develop stronger trust in the coach and to more effectively synthesize feedback due to a more positive communicative environment.

Every conversation in the reverberation cycle begins by identifying the *why*, or *purpose*, as the cycle refers to it. This must take place before addressing any problem—or *what*—as the problem will lack context and framing if the purpose isn't first established. The problem is the concept the coach and the teacher explore or solve so they can achieve the goals laid out in the purpose. Finally, proactive planning is the *how* of the cycle, where the coach and the teacher decide on steps they should take to solve the problem to accomplish the goals set in the purpose. Figure 5.1 provides a reverberation-cycle tool template to help guide the coach and the teacher through this process. The reverberation box at the end provides a space for the coach and the teacher to continue the dialogue or record reflections on the feedback they receive. The coach and the teacher can most effectively leverage this tool digitally through a collaborative cloud-based document.

| Cycle Phase | Teacher Feedback | Coach Feedback |
|---|---|---|
| Purpose (why): | | |
| Problem (what): | | |
| Proactive planning (how): | | |
| **Reverberation** | | |
| Teacher:<br><br><br><br>Coach: | | |

**Figure 5.1: Reverberation-cycle tool template.**

*Visit **go.SolutionTree.com/instruction** for a free reproducible version of this figure.*

Figure 5.2 (pages 52–53) offers an example of a filled-in reverberation-cycle tool after one completed round between a teacher and coach. As the cycle is ongoing, teachers and coaches may use additional copies of the tool for each subsequent round of reverberation.

| Cycle Phase | Teacher Feedback | Coach Feedback |
|---|---|---|
| Purpose:<br><br>To facilitate learning in a meaningful way to engage students at high levels of thinking | I believe my administration values this concept, and I'm very excited about exploring ways to improve my instruction. I'd like to have my coach support me in this. | I can see your passion and energy toward teaching and learning and your desire to grow as a facilitator of learning. |
| Problem:<br><br>The school has adopted a project-based learning approach, and the teacher is having difficulty with content connections. | I value the concept of project-based learning, but with the quantity of standards in the scope and sequence and the limited amount of time I have, I'm having difficulty making this shift. | The beauty of project-based learning is that content standards become more meaningful in the context of a real-world project. I've noticed that you become overwhelmed in planning because of your struggle with making this shift. As we work together, let's look for innovative ways to reduce time and integrate content standards. |
| Proactive planning:<br>1. Collaborative project planning will occur with the coach and the grade-level team.<br>2. The coach will co-teach or model a learning block that includes explicit instruction and student collaboration.<br>3. The coach and the teacher will debrief and reflect on successes and failures. | Planning with my team was extremely valuable. My coach facilitated our planning meeting to ensure we were fully supported as we addressed the challenges of project-based learning. I'm looking forward to my coach modeling a lesson, as I believe it will provide confidence and activate my own prior knowledge for best instructional practices. | I am looking forward to debriefing after the lesson. I want to ensure I receive feedback as well so we can work together to create evidence of high-quality student learning experiences. |

| Reverberation |
| --- |
| Teacher: I really appreciate my coach's support and guidance. During my observation of my coach teaching the lesson, I was better able to see how the whole-group instruction (a minilesson tied to content standards) connected to the small-group project work (student collaboration and critical thinking). My coach was attentive to my needs, transparent about her own experiences, and very encouraging throughout this process. |
| Coach: The teacher was very receptive to new ideas. I think sharing my own experiences and struggles in the classroom helped build the level of camaraderie for us to move forward in our collaboration. |

**Figure 5.2: Sample completed reverberation-cycle tool.**

Notice that this example lists the project-based learning initiative in the problem and not in the purpose. Schools will have many initiatives, and they should view them in terms of the *what* and not the *why*. Within those initiatives, teachers will develop specific goals (the purpose) to help support the vision of engaging students at high levels. It's important to remember that goals should focus on student learning. In *What Doesn't Work in Education: The Politics of Distraction*, Hattie (2015) makes a compelling argument that school leaders spend more time than they should focusing on teachers, when they should focus on students.

It's crucial that the teacher and the coach revisit the purpose, as they will find other problems and concepts arise as they try new things and explore new ways of teaching. They can add new rows to the template as they discover new problems. It's also important for both the teacher and coach to provide feedback to each other (via the reverberation-cycle tool template), keeping the channel of communication consistently open to ensure they continually discover learning opportunities. To ensure a successful reverberation cycle, a coach must establish necessary conditions, ensure productive reflection, and understand and communicate the teacher's role in the process. The following sections will examine these items.

## Necessary Conditions for Successful Reverberation

Before utilizing the reverberation-cycle tool, the coach needs to set the stage for feedback as his or her first step. A possible starter question is, "I know you want to become the most effective teacher possible, and I hope I can support you to become just that. Do you mind if we chat specifically about how we will use feedback to help us both learn and grow together?" This sets the tone for a nonthreatening, trusting, and collaborative conversation.

Reverberation requires that schools and districts establish and nurture feedback communities that make collaboration with other coaches and teachers an expectation and a safe, normal, and critical part of the teaching profession and of the school and district culture. An impactful and reverberating coaching approach necessitates that we re-examine the traditional coaching model cycle that includes preconferences, observations, postconferences, and so on. Coaching can and should follow different pathways, including the incorporation of partnership principles and lesson-study principles (Knight, 2007). The impact of coaching will also expand when we leverage the power of metafeedback (feedback about the feedback process), providing opportunities for the coach, the coachee, and the broader coaching community to contribute metafeedback. The promise of metafeedback is enhanced by the possibilities of coaching in a digital world, in which technological platforms allow for asynchronous coaching and conversations and for easy access to classroom life via video. Successful feedback requires that coaching exists as a positive, ubiquitous part of the teaching profession, not as a feature of evaluation or as a consequence of subpar teaching—we all benefit from coaching.

As Hattie and Yates (2014) stress, feedback is not an isolated classroom event. They focus on feedback from teacher to student, but the same principles can apply to coaching support, as teachers are learners. Hattie and Yates (2014) identify the following nine key points to ensuring effective feedback. To illuminate application to the coach-teacher dynamic, I've made minor adjustments in brackets:

1. The feedback process resides in that what is received and interpreted by a [teacher], rather than what a [coach] gives or believes has taken place.

2. Feedback can work best when criteria for success are known to the [teacher] in advance, and where the goal to achieve such success is shared by [teacher] and [coach] alike.

3. Feedback can best cue attention onto a task, with a known goal or sub goal, and away from self-focus.

4. Feedback must engage a learner at, or just above, the current level of functioning [defined by the current level of teacher practice].

5. Feedback must challenge the [teacher] to invest effort in moving forwards, and assure the [teacher] that it is perfectly natural to experience difficulties when mastering difficult tasks.

6. Feedback is powerful when the [building] climate is one of welcoming errors and seeing disconfirmation as a natural and positive part of developing and exercising new skills.

7. It is optimal when feedback matches the content of the instruction given earlier, and is in accord with available social modelling stimuli identified as worthy of emulation.

8. Feedback thrives in an environment where errors are welcomed, and error training may be a worthwhile adjunct to increase the power of feedback.

9. Feedback is received and used by [teachers] when [coaches] themselves are prepared to adapt and adjust their methods and priorities in response to the outcomes indexed through [teachers'] success on various [teacher measures]. (p. 55)

## Productive Reflection

Throughout the reverberation cycle, both teachers and coaches solve problems related to an overarching purpose or goal, providing feedback to each other along the way. Because many conversations about a particular lesson or instructional practice can happen over a period of time, it helps to synthesize the interactions into reflective takeaways. I suggest teachers and coaches use the reflection tools in figures 5.3 and 5.4 (pages 56–57) to support their reflections on a weekly basis. This ensures the conversations are actionable and they do not get lost in an amalgamation of thoughts and suggestions.

To promote accountability and transparency, all teachers should have the ability to see the completed coach reflection (via a shared, collaborative, cloud-based document), but the teacher reflection tool should be visible only to the coach. The coach should have access to each individual teacher reflection tool via a shared, cloud-based folder. The reflection tool's simple design and explicit prompts provide teachers with a quick and easy summative reflection that aids in decision making.

## Teacher's Role in Reverberation

The beauty of the reverberation cycle is that it provides an open invitation to two-way discourse not just during a debrief. Reverberation can occur asynchronously through a collaborative digital document or synchronously through an impromptu conversation. The invitation is framed around the premise that the coach and the teacher work together toward the same ultimate goal. However, teachers may find it unnatural to provide a colleague with continual feedback unless they are intentionally prompted to do so. Coaches must continually ask for and seek feedback from teachers to establish this practice as a natural collaborative norm. We all see things through different lenses; therefore, the teacher and the coach have an invaluable opportunity to grow as feedback providers throughout the reverberation process.

| Coach Reflection | |
|---|---|
| **Week of:** _____ | |

| Prompt | Response |
|---|---|
| How could I have made _____ more engaging? | |
| Based on what happened this week, what will I change next week? | |
| How did my colleagues push my thinking? | |
| What was something risky I tried that worked? | |
| What long-term goals have I not made progress with? What will I do about that? | |

**Figure 5.3: Coach reflection tool.**

*Visit* **go.SolutionTree.com/instruction** *for a free reproducible version of this figure.*

| | |
|---|---|
| **Teacher Reflection** | |

Teacher's name: _____

Week of: _____

| Prompt | Response |
|---|---|
| _____ <br> would have been more engaging if . . . | |
| Based on what happened this week, I hope next week, we will . . . | |
| My coach pushed my thinking by . . . | |
| Something risky I tried that worked was . . . | |
| Some long-term goals I don't feel I've made progress on are . . . <br><br> I will address this by . . . | |

**Figure 5.4: Teacher reflection tool.**

*Visit **go.SolutionTree.com/instruction** for a free reproducible version of this figure.*

Additionally, the reverberation process doesn't only have to reside between a teacher and a coach; it can also involve interactions between teachers without the facilitation of the coach. While people may not always have the ability to accurately judge their own aptitudes, they are usually quite good when it comes to critiquing others' competencies. Encourage teachers to invite fellow teachers, with whom they have already established mutual trust and respect, into the classroom for an informal observation or to engage in the reverberation cycle. These trusted teachers can provide additional helpful and specific feedback to the teacher they observe.

Coaches may find it daunting not only to encourage teachers to give them feedback but also to create the congenial relationship necessary for effective and meaningful coaching. It may seem that building high-quality connections would require months of friendship. However, in her book *Energize Your Workplace*, University of Michigan professor Jane Dutton (2003) finds that "high-quality connections don't require 'a deep or intimate relationship'" (as cited in DeWitt & Lang, 2016). Peter DeWitt and Nathan Lang (2016) further assert, "A single interaction marked by respect, trust, and mutual engagement is enough to generate energy for both people. So even though it may appear short-lived, don't [trivialize] those connections. These small moments of connection have exponentially high relational impacts." Also, these connections will support an environment for two-way reverberation. The following sections in this chapter will further examine ways in which coaches promote a culture of transparent and productive feedback.

## Praise and Affirmation Versus Feedback

Many times, coaches think they are giving feedback when they are really just giving praise. As discussed in chapter 4 (page 37), praise plays a very valuable part in discourse; it creates a foundation conducive to an effective reverberation cycle. Praise often takes the form of short affirmations that are not necessarily descriptive or specific. Coaches may walk through a classroom to pat a teacher on the back; tell him or her, "Awesome job"; or give him or her a thumbs-up as a means of praise. They may even provide the teacher with an email or a sticky note that states, "I loved being in your classroom" (DeWitt & Lang, 2016). When teachers receive this kind of praise, it becomes evident that these walk-throughs don't make up part of any focused effort centered on improving practice. DeWitt and Lang (2016) recommend that before and after a walkthrough, coaches and teachers work together to identify look-fors that should occur in the classroom, and have a dialogue focused specifically on the feedback they receive from the walkthrough.

Feedback has a much different purpose than praise. While the goals of praise and feedback are inherently similar (to genuinely increase professional growth), DeWitt and Lang (2016) explain that "feedback needs to be specific and timely, and it's even more powerful when it's focused on a specific goal." This does not mean every teacher conversation must center on feedback. However, it *does* mean coaches must make their feedback explicit when they do give it. Following the reverberation cycle helps focus feedback on specific goals or a purpose.

## Informal Dialogue in Debriefing

Coaches shouldn't always give feedback in a formal debrief or a formal sit-down, as these can create stress or anxiety for the teacher. As coaches schedule time to share feedback, using the words *meeting* and *conversation* can cause teachers to have negative or guarded feelings. Conversation starters can help facilitate an informal dialogue. DeWitt and Lang (2016) recommend, "Instead try a simple and polite 'Let's chat about how I can support you.' This language dismantles whatever concoction of negative self-talk that may be developing in the mind of the teacher." Additionally, coaches can use a collaborative, digitally shared document such as the reverberation-cycle tool (see figure 5.1, page 51) to provide useful opportunities for asynchronous reverberation in a nonthreatening environment.

Most often, a coach will start the informal debrief dialogue by asking, "How do you think the lesson went?" Many times, teachers' responses will go one of two directions.

1. **Response A:** "It went really well!" As humans, we have the inclination to talk about how well something went. According to Justin Kruger and David Dunning (1999), we possess bias known as *illusory superiority*, where we tend to overestimate our own qualities and abilities relative to others'. This effect will distort what actually happened and won't give us an accurate picture.

2. **Response B:** "It went well but could have gone better if I . . ." It has often been my observation that, as educators who are concerned about perception, we don't want to come across as unteachable or unable to grow, so we throw in some humility. Even the most genuine and sincere responses to the aforementioned question don't get us to the heart of the conversation that needs to happen.

Although kind and collegial, these responses don't fully yield the most effective or productive debriefing conversations. When beginning a debrief conversation, acknowledge a teacher's passion and your role in supporting him or her. Always begin with the *why* or purpose. Your coaching notes during a classroom observation should relate back to the purpose and the identified problem. During a debrief, these will help you stay focused on the conversation. Questions such as the following will keep the conversation focused on specific goals identified in the reverberation process.

- "How did you tackle the problem we identified?"
- "Did you find our planning helpful in achieving the purpose?"
- "What evidence did you gather that shows students engaged in high-level thinking and learning?"

Another great conversation starter is, "How did you reflect on the lesson?" This places the emphasis not on ability or perceived experience but on self-reflection for the sole purpose of growth. Additionally, this opens the door to conversations about metacognitive processes, inclusion of student feedback, and trusted peer observations.

Another option that can help move dialogue into an informal realm is to rethink where the coach and the teacher have these conversations and to initiate *moving chats*. As the name suggests, moving chats happen during a casual walk or just in a new meeting place for a change in scenery. Moving chats particularly help lower the guard a teacher puts up or alleviate any anxiety a teacher has going into a debrief. Think about times when you found it easiest to share and reflect. You probably weren't in a fluorescent office with someone staring directly at you. You probably spoke on a leisurely walk, in a relaxed coffee shop, or in another comfortable setting. A nice, easy walking pace even induces a higher mental alertness (Rhodes, n.d.). Walk the halls, the gym, outside, or wherever your chat can stay conversational, focused, and comfortable.

## Professional Growth for Coaches

It's difficult to quantify or qualify your own success as a coach. However, reverberation practices not only strengthen teacher practice but provide opportunities for coaches to further their own professional growth and development and gain feedback on their work. While building administrators may be too evaluative or critical or may provide a falsely illusory and utopian perspective, coaches can find other opportunities to receive coaching by seeking out some surprising sources: fellow coaches and teachers, their students, and even other coaches from different contexts. Social media has also opened up vast opportunities for coaches to establish professional learning networks. Virtual interactions can lead to deeper relationships that can develop into reverberation cycles and feedback conversations. Twitter is one of the best places to start. Look for education-focused hashtags (for example, #edchat, #leadupchat, and #diverged). Even though many coaches are tied to building test scores or principal observations, they truly hold a unique position to cultivate tangible evidence of growth.

## Conclusion

Feedback that seeks to correct or evaluate a teacher becomes destructive, especially when feedback processes seem secretive due to poor communication. Furthermore, secretive practices create a guarded culture. If teachers are guarded, they won't provide feedback, and their reverberation cycle will only become as effective as their guarded culture. A coach's role is not only to empower a powerful feedback process but also to promote a culture of trust, transparency, vulnerability, and sincerity.

The reverberation cycle represents not only changing reflective feedback processes but also providing new tools to ensure fidelity to the processes. Coaches frame feedback as reverberation to establish a consistent and safe culture of two-way feedback so that we may change and grow as educators. When we view feedback as possible truths grounded in validity, we can welcome it as an opportunity to see teaching, learning, and professional growth in new ways.

# SIX

♥

# SINCERITY

Sincerity drives coaches to become the best versions of themselves and encourage teachers to do the same by illuminating
teacher voice and supporting teacher innovation and creativity.

While people often use the terms *sincerity* and *authenticity* in tandem, *authenticity* has become exhaustingly overused in many social contexts, including the
realm of education. It's often touted as being a collaborative group norm for
teachers to abide by, but it can be difficult to implement with fidelity, especially
if the building culture doesn't promote it. While both terms have roots in the
same context of revealing truth, people use *authenticity* to define both objects
and human behavior, and people mainly use *sincerity* to define the human con-
dition. For example, you hear about Mexican food being authentic, but you
wouldn't hear people describe it as *sincere*. I define *sincerity* as a personality
trait used to describe transparent and truthful people who have the ability to
self-monitor their interactions. Coaches must display sincerity as they support
teachers in illuminating their voice, fostering creativity and innovation, and
promoting values-based decision making. Because the term *authenticity* per-
vades societal constructs and much of the important research discussed in this
chapter, you'll see references to both authenticity and sincerity in this chapter,
but for the purposes of this book and coaching work in general, I prefer the
term *sincerity*.

According to Steven W. Gangestad and Mark Snyder (2000), our level of
sincerity depends on our level of a trait called *self-monitoring*. As coaches lead
with sincerity, they must find the appropriate balance of self-monitoring. If a
person's self-monitoring is low, it allows his or her current state to drive his or
her decisions, no matter the environmental circumstances, and other people

may label him or her impulsive. If a person's self-monitoring is high, he or she excessively filters actions based on environmental circumstances, and others might label him or her fake. A coach's self-monitoring will be higher when he or she perceives a teacher as frustrated after a challenging student interaction than if the coach and the teacher casually chatted at an after-school event. When thinking about a healthy balance of self-monitoring, it's important for coaches to ask themselves, To what extent is the decision or action I want to make motivated by how I feel in the moment? To what extent is the decision or action motivated by making another person react positively? Can I make a decision that takes into account my own perception but at the same time validates the other person's perception?

The ability to effectively self-monitor hinges on a coach's level of *withitness*. Researcher Jacob Kounin (1970) coined the term *withitness* as a way to describe how most effective teachers regularly monitor classroom behaviors. For the purposes of this book, *withitness* refers to coaches' ability to sync up with teachers' emotions and behaviors.

Leading with authenticity helps one focus on positive achievements, rather than flaws (Jensen & Luthans, 2006; Peterson & Luthans, 2003), and advances team members' trust, which results in emotional security and innovative thinking (Avolio, Gardner, Walumbwa, Luthans, & May, 2004). In this chapter, we will explore the concept of sincerity and how, when combined with self-monitoring and withitness, it can help coaches illuminate teacher voice and support creativity and innovation.

## Illuminating Teacher Voice

Nathanael J. Fast, Ethan R. Burris, and Caroline A. Bartel (2014) reveal that "incorporating employee voice is essential to organizational performance" (p. 1013), yet many leaders struggle with incorporating input from subordinates. Teachers may hesitate to share ideas if school leaders and coaches become defensive to teachers' ideas due to their own insecurities. However, when coaches communicate and act from a place of sincerity, it gives teachers permission to question and challenge coaches, even out in the open.

Sincerity is not a static, one-time positive interaction but a dynamic cultural norm, and it means taking a consistent and active interest in others' voices. When coaches display sincere actions inconsistently, they don't promote a no-holds-barred approach to illuminating teacher voice. Additionally, sincerity requires more than just giving teachers a platform to express their opinions and ideas and hearing them out. It requires *active* listening in which coaches take a genuine interest in seeking out and understanding diverse viewpoints while keeping an open mind. Illuminating teachers' voices creates opportunities to learn and grow from each other. At the heart of successful illumination of teacher voice (and corresponding school culture) is the belief that you can learn something from everyone around you, regardless of position, background, or experience. It has been my experience that, without this core belief of sincerity present, teachers will not voice their opinions, concerns, and goals because they won't feel sincerely valued.

Russell J. Quaglia developed a school voice model (Quaglia Institute for School Voice and Aspirations, n.d.), based on thirty years of research, that provides a vehicle through which the members of the school community can ensure everyone hears, respects, and values their voices. Generally speaking, in this model, everyone within the school community has a shared responsibility to continually improve education, sincerely value every voice, and capitalize on every individual's unique skills and talents (Quaglia Institute for School Voice and Aspirations, n.d.). This model supports having a healthy balance of self-monitoring and highly focused withitness. The model comprises three components: (1) listening, (2) learning, and (3) leading. Listening must be active, and it must aim to seek out other people's opinions and beliefs. Learning means developing an understanding of others' points of view—not only teachers' and principal's but also students' and parents'. Leading involves analyzing stakeholders' collective ideas and acting on those ideas through decision making.

Inspired by the school voice model, I created the voice-leveraging tool in figure 6.1 (pages 66–67) to assist coaches in displaying sincerity through their decision making and leadership. The tool serves as a guide for coaches in the discovery of an issue, a struggle, or a potential demand for change that comes out on an initial conversation or interview with stakeholders. This interview or conversation accounts for the Listen portion of the school voice model, during which coaches take notes. The voice-leveraging tool supports the Learn and Lead components as coaches extract and synthesize the takeaways they identify from these conversations. Coaches then share their discoveries with leadership at the conclusion of the process of using this tool. Figure 6.1 provides an example of a coach using the tool for guidance in identifying an instructional challenge, listening to others' viewpoints, learning from the viewpoints, and then determining next steps in leading literacy instruction.

The coach in figure 6.1 effectively led and supported teachers and students with sincerity by listening to and learning from others before taking action. Oftentimes, coaches react quickly if they feel they already have a predetermined solution. The process of using this tool illustrates the importance of not jumping into creating a solution prematurely and instead consulting and considering teachers' voices—as well as all other stakeholders' voices—in decision making.

**Narrative From Coach**

*The focus of my professional development sessions for the fall semester has been on literacy instruction and strategies, but through my observations, I've noticed that when students engage in independent reading, they don't consistently apply the strategies (previously modeled by the teacher) by themselves, nor make meaning of unfamiliar contexts. Students aren't using the cues themselves to recognize how the new context connects to prior learning.*

**Learn**

Record viewpoints from students, parents, teachers, and administrators. Additionally, reflect on any research conclusions.

- *Students: Students say they enjoy reading books they choose but don't often find a connection to what they're reading for independent practice and the texts the teacher chooses.*

- *Parents: Parents are unaware of any cues or exercises their children use in class.*

- *Teachers: Transfer of skills is more successful when teachers use protocols or some structured framework. Procedures and memorization of steps haven't had success with students.*

- *Administrators: Administrators believe teachers are overusing scaffolding and supports.*

Connection to research or prior work: *I read and reflected on a journal article written by Grant Wiggins (2010) on the authentic transfer of learning.*

**Lead**

Record goals and actions to take based on understanding of multiple viewpoints.

Goals: *I need to create professional learning opportunities for teachers that support their literacy instruction in how to apply skill sets from one reading experience to another.*

Actions: *Provide teachers with the following instructional strategies to support student-learning transfer.*

- *Think-alouds and explicit reminders of what students are now doing and its purpose*

- *Opportunities for students to apply skills in a new context*

- *Essential questions that suggest the kinds of connections students will have to make throughout their reading and creation processes (If students have awareness that essential questions will be used to explore connections between learning experiences, they will more likely make connections on their own.)*

> • *Opportunities to practice judgment, not just skill (Transfer is about judging which skill and knowledge to use when. Teachers should give students opportunities to practice and get feedback on their attempts to judge which skill or knowledge they might best use in different contexts. Have learners do think-alouds and provide reports of why they did what they did when they did it. Learning to self-monitor in this way improves both self-assessment and self-adjustment.)*

*Source: Adapted from Wiggins, 2010.*

**Figure 6.1: Sample voice-leveraging tool.**

*Visit* **go.SolutionTree.com/instruction** *for a free reproducible version of this figure.*

# Supporting Teacher Creativity and Innovation

Creativity and innovation flourish in environments where teammates view their leaders as sincere because they exhibit authentic leadership. But as a leader or a coach, just saying or believing you are being authentic doesn't automatically translate to building creativity inside your teams. In fact, research (Černe, Jaklič, & Škerlavaj, 2013) shows leaders' perception of their own authentic leadership and others' perception of their authentic leadership have different effects. Researchers Matej Černe, Marko Jaklič, and Miha Škerlavaj (2013) have investigated a supervisor's influence on a subordinate's creativity and innovation. The research finds that team leaders' self-ascribed authentic leadership does not influence either individual creativity or team innovation, whereas the opposite holds true for perceived authentic leadership. In other words, a leader's self-assessment and awareness of his or her goals, emotions, values, and motives does not have an impact on individual creativity and team innovation, but others' perceptions of the leader's level of authenticity does. Leaders need to demonstrate awareness to others in a way that his or her followers perceive he or she possesses that characteristic (Černe et al., 2013). In this study, Černe et al. (2013) state how team leaders can clearly present their authenticity to others on their team:

> Leaders must exhibit transparent relations with the employees and demonstrate high moral level, thus inspiring team members to follow their lead (Novicevic, Davis, Dorn, Buckley, & Brown, 2005) . . . and suggest novel ideas, which are also more likely to be put to successful use. (p. 65)

Only then can authentic leaders inspire creativity and innovation. With this information, coaches must shift their focus from self-ascribed authenticity to perceived authenticity. Once teachers perceive a coach as being authentic, the school environment will be primed for creativity and innovation. The following sections will focus on three innovative strategies that coaches can focus on to foster creativity and innovation: (1) understanding teachers' goals, (2) analyzing and making decisions based on teachers' value systems, and (3) embracing strategic waiting.

## Understanding Teachers' Goals

As previous chapters have noted, coaches are integral in facilitating the collaborative process of goal development that supports teachers' and students' growth. However, teachers will still develop some personal goals without direct influence from a coach—goals that they derive from personal ambitions and interests. Sincere coaches best support teachers if they not only have awareness of teachers' self-initiated goals but also have the ability to provide feedback on the goals. A brief from the Quaglia Institute for School Voice and Aspirations (2016) explains that many teachers don't feel their leaders know their individual goals. When teachers have coaches who engage with them and their respective goals, it helps teachers feel valued, and it empowers teacher voice.

## Analyzing and Making Decisions Based on Teachers' Value Systems

Because schools are made up of humans with all different backgrounds and perspectives, coaches must form a good understanding of the varying worldviews and value systems of the teachers they work with. The human development theory of spiral dynamics (Beck & Cowan, 1996; Graves & Lee, 2004) provides a foundation that can help us understand others' belief paradigms and behaviors and become more sincere in our work so we stimulate their creativity and innovation. Spiral dynamics is a theory Don Beck and Christopher Cowan developed and refined, based on the late psychologist Clare Graves' unpublished works. The theory is so named because of what it identifies as humans' ever-developing and changing worldviews and personalities—which are constantly spiraling as peoples' experiences reshape their ideas and beliefs. Because sincerity is deeply rooted in social and personal worldviews, unpacking the spiral dynamics theory is beneficial in our use of sincerity as a driver. Leveraging sincerity to illuminate diverse perspectives, personalities, backgrounds, and learning styles is vital for spawning creativity and innovation in the classroom.

Beck and Cowan (1996) use the term *meme* (also referred to as *valueMEME*) to represent a paradigm, belief, or value system. This term originates from the word *memetics*, an evolutionary model of cultural information transfer. While earlier versions of this theory use the term *MEME^*, and Beck and Cowan (1996) oscillate between the terms *meme* and *valueMEME*, all three terms represent the same ideas. For simplicity, I will use *meme* in this book to refer to this aspect of spiral dynamics. Beck and Cowan (1996) categorize memes into color-coded hierarchical levels or tiers that differ qualitatively and quantitatively and are arranged around personal evolutionary development. For example, the red meme describes the value system of someone who is assertive and who pursues dominance. The blue meme is characterized by obedience and compliance. The green meme is relativistic and communal, and individuals whom this meme represents work together toward the common good in a cooperative manner. Memes are organized into two tiers. The first-tier memes are associated with the concepts of having, wanting, getting, and acting in ways to end feelings of shortcoming or failure. The second tier represents evolutionary development that takes one beyond living in fear. Second-tier thinking manifests in people as a high degree of sincere self-acceptance and a high capacity for compassion for others. Figure 6.2 highlights the memes from a lower to a higher progression (Roemischer, 2002). Visit **go.SolutionTree.com/instruction** for live links to comprehensive, color-coded visuals of these memes.

| | Meme Color and Classification | Basic Theme |
|---|---|---|
| **Second-Tier Meme** | **Yellow: Systemic or Integrative** | Embrace the fact that chaos exists and it requires flexibility, spontaneity, and systems thinking. |
| **First-Tier Memes** | **Green: Communitarian or Egalitarian** | Seek peace within the inner self and explore, with others, the caring dimensions of community. |
| | **Orange: Goal-Oriented or Strategic** | Act in your own self-interest by playing the game to win. |
| | **Blue: Purposeful or Authoritarian** | Life has meaning, direction, and purpose with predetermined outcomes. |
| | **Red: Impulsive or Assertive** | Be what you are and do what you want, regardless. |
| | **Purple: Magical or Animistic** | Keep the spirits happy and the tribe's nest warm and safe. |
| | **Beige: Instinctive or Survivalistic** | Do what you must just to stay alive. |

*Source: Adapted from Roemischer, 2002, pp. 7–8.*

**Figure 6.2: Tiered memes.**

Spiral dynamics theorizes that additional higher color levels will develop as humans continue to advance and new experiences allow the further evolution of thought processes. For example, a turquoise level is beginning to emerge in the second tier above the yellow level. This level represents a holistic meme with a mindset of wholeness, balance, and intuitive thinking. Additional levels that will emerge transcend humans' current level of understanding of the world. The possibilities for the future are endless!

Although spiral dynamics hierarchically orders the memes by thinking tiers, coaches should not place a value judgment on teachers based on their current levels. Experiences over time will contribute to an evolution of personal beliefs and attitudes and influence the meme a person identifies with. Think of the colors as representative buckets that shape worldviews, and not necessarily that represent the beliefs themselves. (For example, you may like exercise because you want your heart to be healthy, but someone else may like exercise because he or she desires a certain physique. The belief that exercise is important is the same, but the worldviews that shape that belief are different.) The population a coach works with will represent a distribution of colors, so it's important to recognize that varying levels exist and can help inform how we think and work together. With a deeper understanding of the values-based thinking styles that exist in the school community, we will better plan for collaborative sessions focused on creativity and innovation. A coach displaying sincerity can consider the personalities of the teachers in a building and the disbursement of memes among those teachers, in order to anticipate faculty reactions to new initiatives. This enables the coach to aid leaders in deciding whether a respective worldview, action, or initiative will cause negative visceral reactions by teachers or provide an inspirational springboard for their next big step.

Initiatives and change efforts often fail because the leaders focus on themselves and what makes them tick, and they assume teachers and students share their same value system. Many times, we, as coaches, ask, "How can we create buy-in?" or "How can we convince teachers to change?" If we display sincerity in our coaching role, we must approach our relational work differently. We should focus on how our actions connect to others' intrinsic motivational flows. For example, teachers functioning at higher color levels will likely have more options and a higher sense of freedom than those at lower color levels because their specific values or worldviews make them better able to choose one instructional strategy over another or embrace an innovative idea over a stagnant one. Just as we understand the value of differentiated instruction because students learn in different ways, we must also apply the same understanding to the ways we learn as adults. As coaches, we must focus on facilitating meaningful connections among teachers, students, instructional strategies, learning experiences, and tools. We can successfully make these connections when we understand how learners think, learn, and adapt to change. Change requires us to evolve, and therefore, we must create innovative ways to support teachers based on who they have become in the midst of new circumstances.

As coaches look to support teacher creativity and innovation, they should take more interest in providing differentiated and varied ways of thinking than in categorizing teachers by a static color and only working within that domain. People are creative at different levels based on certain values and worldviews, and they will move in and out of memes based on changing environmental factors or because certain events lead to an evolution of thinking. The coach should be aware of this and provide options for how teachers can come up with different solutions and creative and innovative instructional approaches. Using the idea-generation tool in figure 6.3 (page 72), the coach facilitates a protocol to allow teachers to begin at a level that most resonates with how they think and learn. (Note that the beige level is absent, as our modern lives allow us the luxury of thinking beyond mere survival.) The prompts in the figure align with respective color memes, and the goal is for teachers to move toward the higher-tiered yellow meme as their thinking evolves over time. While the goal is to progress, this is not to say that a lower meme means a teacher is less advanced as a teacher. It simply reflects that he or she is less advanced on the color scale.

Before the idea-generation activity, the coach determines some initial grouping possibilities based on previous observation data and conversations, but allows for a flexible starting point each time he or she uses the tool or activity. In the sample work scenario in figure 6.3, the coach has brought forth an idea that would change the way teachers plan lessons. In this scenario, lesson planning has become exhaustive for teachers, and data show that the amount of time teachers spend planning has not yielded the high levels of learning expected. Additionally, the teachers have had lesson planning in place for decades, and the team is considering a new way of collaborating. A coach can use the tool in figure 6.3 for any change initiative by replacing the lesson-planning content with another topic.

| Meme | Prompt |
|------|--------|
| **Yellow:** Systemic or Integrative | (Work alone.) Choose the most transformational idea you generated from any of the other meme's prompts you have previously worked with. Deconstruct and add components, and then resynthesize them in a way that will improve the idea. Justify why you think this new improvement would work better. |
| **Green:** Communitarian or Egalitarian | (Work in a group.) Share your innovative ideas so far with your team. As a group, actively listen, learn, and then build on all these ideas to come up with more innovative suggestions. |
| **Orange:** Goal-Oriented or Strategic | (Work alone.) What risks would you willingly take to create an innovative lesson-planning process? Include a mix of current norms and new norms. |
| **Blue:** Purposeful or Authoritarian | (Work in a group.) What agreed-on norms and processes surround lesson planning? Come up with some ideas together to demonstrate your thinking. |
| **Red:** Impulsive or Assertive | (Work alone.) If funds and resources were not a concern and the sky was the limit, what unique, individual take would you have on lesson planning? Generate ideas. |
| **Purple:** Magical or Animistic | (Work in a group.) What's the most basic lesson-planning template to express your school's vision of instruction? Generate some ideas to demonstrate your thinking. |

**Figure 6.3: Differentiated idea-generation tool (lesson-planning example).**

Coaches can use this tool and the holistic spiral-dynamics approach not only to spawn creativity and innovation but also to create a consistent and systemic way to approach all issues in leading assessment, curriculum, instruction, learning, professional development, and so on. That way, all these elements connect together in a meaningful, authentic, and sincere fashion.

## Embracing Strategic Waiting

A third strategy that can support a coach's sincere efforts to encourage creativity and innovation is something I call *strategic waiting*—a term closely related to *procrastination* but with a more positive implication. We all procrastinate at some level, and some of us do this more than others. Procrastination has taken on a stigma, as it gets associated with subpar work or ineffective prioritizing. However, Grant (2016) contends that procrastination inspires innovation and creativity, because it allows a person's mind to wander, leading to more divergent thinking. He shares that while many of the greatest products in human history resulted from years of meticulous rewrites and revisions, some resulted from procrastination, including Martin Luther King Jr.'s "I Have a Dream" speech, Abraham Lincoln's Gettysburg Address, and Leonardo da Vinci's *Mona Lisa*. Creating at the last minute allows for flexibility to improvise in the moment, as opposed to setting a script in stone weeks in advance.

Strategic waiting means *intentionally* not acting on a task or project that one needs to complete, increasing the creativity and innovation of the final product by letting it ruminate and allowing more experiences to shape one's thinking. An example of applying strategic waiting to educational practices comes in the common task of lesson planning. Coaches sometimes ask teachers to submit lesson plans far in advance, and they expect those teachers to execute the plans exactly as the submissions describe; however, this practice does not support creativity and innovation. Alternatively, coaches can support teachers in strategic waiting by asking teachers to share upcoming tasks with them (not in the form of a structured lesson plan) and giving them the freedom to adapt the tasks before and during instruction. Coaches can then follow up with the teachers through informal (but consistent) conversations to ask how external stimuli, dialogue with colleagues, or self-reflection changed the substance of the work itself; how teachers will approach their work differently as a result; or how they might measure the effectiveness of their work differently.

Coaches can use the guide in figure 6.4 (page 74) to support teachers' strategic waiting. This guide helps illuminate how tasks change over time to create a better outcome. You can also use this guide as a collaboratively shared digital document. In the first box, simply record the original task (such as "Create a schedule for observation preconferences," "Create a small group rotation schedule," and so on). In the second box, record external stimuli that influenced how you approached the task (for example, "Had a conversation with teacher in the hall," "Read intriguing book on small-group instruction," and so on). In the third box, record any ways external stimuli changed the original task into something more useful. In the fourth box, record how strategic waiting improved the original task.

**Directions:** Use this template to guide you through the process of strategic waiting.

Original task:

Stimulus:

Stimulus:

Stimulus:

Change or changes in the following:

Purpose of the task:

Content of the task:

Manifestation of the task:

Measurement of task effectiveness:

Reflection (Did strategic waiting prove more successful?):

**Figure 6.4: Strategic-waiting guide.**

*Visit* **go.SolutionTree.com/instruction** *for a free reproducible version of this figure.*

Some highly sensitive tasks, such as responding to urgent student behavior matters, school safety, and so on, of course, require immediate action. With other tasks, such as lesson planning, strategic waiting can result in more malleable and meaningful instruction. In a culture of collaboration and sincerity, teachers, principals, and coaches can proudly admit to each other that they strategically wait on certain tasks to allow for greater creativity and innovation.

## Conclusion

As coaches, we must possess sincerity because we can't always objectively judge our own authenticity, and even when we accurately rate ourselves as authentic, it won't inspire others to be creative and innovative. But when our colleagues perceive us as sincere, we are able to be fully flexible and agile in our collaborative working relationships. When both the communicator and the receiver perceive communication as sincere, it gives permission for them both to question and challenge one another.

Sincere coaches care deeply about their work and their personal and professional growth goals. They also deeply care about teachers' and students' goals. Sincere coaches pay attention to how they present themselves and how others perceive them and then strive to behave like the people they claim to be. Their actions and efforts reflect the values of the education profession. By relating to others' worldviews and values, coaches can speak honestly without making others feel uncomfortable, articulate their thinking without attacking someone's character, promote learning without judgment, and share their thoughts that might differ from others' thoughts in a mutually respectful environment.

School teams will continue to face challenges and struggle if school leaders manage them in traditional ways. Our goal is not to manage people, nor to focus our work on ensuring a school's function is to solely operate for productivity and efficiency. Just as our students have changed in the way they think and what they value, the same holds true for adult learners; therefore, illuminating teacher and student voices carries more importance than ever before. What we feel, think, and believe about education and learning shifts and changes depending on what we teach, where we teach, and whom we teach with. As our values change, so do our actions, and sincerity affects the degree to which our coaching connects teachers' and students' values to their actions.

# SEVEN

# INFLUENCE

Coaches can use their influence to create demand for, inspire, and catalyze change.

Effective coaches use the influence they have cultivated through the relationships they have built to affect change or advocate for positive change. They leverage trusting, positive relationships and their unique partnership role to catalyze change. Additionally, they support divergent ideas for the sake of growth in a dynamically changing educational landscape. An effective change process must move from the realm of abstract ideas to concrete actions.

When implementing change, coaches should have an acute awareness of the demand for that change and their own vision, purpose, and inspiration. This encompasses what Sinek (2009) refers to as the *why*. When strategizing how we, as coaches, will get our colleagues to change, we often start with the *why*. Starting with the *why* is a great strategy and has a lot of merit in many change efforts. But when innovators advocate for change and explain their why, they run the risk of clashing with deep-seated convictions, as they cause others to question their common notions of what's possible (Grant, 2016). In his book *Originals*, Grant (2016) illustrates an example of this notion through the story of a college senior, Meredith Perry, who was compelled to innovatively create wireless power. Grant (2016) describes how Perry finally succeeded when she did something out of the norm: "she simply stopped telling experts what it was she was trying to create [and] instead of explaining her plan to generate wireless power, she merely provided the specifications of the technology she wanted" (pp. 123–124). In her original pitch, she stated, "'I'm trying to build a transducer to send power over the air.' Her new pitch disguised the purpose: 'I'm looking for someone to design a transducer with these parameters. Can you make this part?'" (Grant, 2016, p. 124). The second approach was more effective because when she didn't specify the new idea, the experts' responses weren't influenced or restricted by the frame of thinking established by existing wired technologies that would impede this innovation. Perry went on to create her own company called uBeam and a device that can wirelessly charge multiple phones simultaneously at a distance of up to ten feet.

In education, we face the daunting task of challenging some deep-rooted traditional practices that have been instilled into the teaching pedigree as far back as the Industrial Revolution. These deeply held practices are stitched into the fabric of teaching, and therefore, teachers feel personally connected to them. When you share your *why* with teachers, they may often meet you with staunch criticism and fear. This doesn't mean we have to stop sharing our novel ideas or that we should change our efforts of sharing our vision of what could be. But it does mean when sharing with our colleagues or pitching to a group of influencers (community members, other school leaders, and so on), we have to share our ideas in a smart and extremely outwardly focused way. And, as with the example of Meredith Perry, it also means we need to home in on the *how* and then gradually illuminate the *why*. Vision statements are grandiose and audacious, so much so that often there is a gap between what our vision calls for and what we actually do to follow that vision (the vision-action gap). Identifying the *why*, the *how*, and the *what* will help close this gap and make action more palpable.

It is crucial that we not only articulate the *why* but also specify the *where*— where we want to end up as a result of our *why*. Without a target in mind, one pathway of change has as much merit as another, and we can consider any change. As education consultants Willard R. Daggett and Richard D. Jones (2014) explain, "Schools need to know where they are going before they try to get there. While this may seem like common sense, most schools do not begin with a clear picture of what their desired student results are" (p. 8). Instead, schools skip to the *what*—the changes and solutions (Daggett & Jones, 2014). If leadership wholeheartedly believes that the level of student learning has direct ties to teacher efficacy, then it should have a focus on adult learning via an empowering instructional coaching framework that delineates the *why*, *where*, *what*, and *how* from the outset.

After we've determined the *why*, *where*, and *what*, we focus on the *how*, and that's the focus of this chapter. Instructional coaches should play a vital role in managing change in their building. Unfortunately, this role often gets placed solely on the school administrators. In a healthy culture of collaborative leadership, the instructional coach can use his or her influence to help lead change, especially in focusing on the *how* of change. In this chapter, we will examine recommended approaches to three specific challenges that coaches commonly face as they attempt to influence change: (1) reframing the focus from ineffective teaching to effective student learning, (2) getting divergent ideas to fly, and (3) moving forward through the unknown.

## Reframing the Focus From Ineffective Teaching to Effective Student Learning

Principals often phrase an elusive but pervasive expectation placed on coaches to help teachers improve their craft as, "Work with this ineffective teacher." How do we define the *ineffective teacher*? Ineffective teachers typically won't admit to themselves that they are ineffective. Many studies have shown that people tend to think they have greater abilities in things—from personality traits, such as intelligence and honesty, to skills, such as driving and academic performance— than they actually do (Ghose, 2013). Given that humans typically have an elevated self-concept, many often find it difficult to seek or receive feedback. But the reality remains that teachers' performance may not be as effective as they perceive it to be, and in order to improve, they must face this hard truth.

Whether coaches want to admit it, how a teacher makes them feel heavily influences a lot of their perceptions about the teacher's effectiveness or ineffectiveness. Many effective teachers come across as direct or abrasive, while many ineffective teachers might make coaches feel happy and enthusiastic. Therefore, coaches have to pinpoint ineffective teachers very specifically, as this specification will affect how the coaches approach and work alongside those teachers. For the coach's purposes, simply stated, the ineffective teacher has not demonstrated success in facilitating and supporting student learning or actively works against the goal of promoting student learning. Coaches can measure this quantitatively and qualitatively using the following data sources: student surveys, classroom observations, peer observations, assessments, and any other instruments used to collect evidence tied to teacher instruction and classroom practices.

School leaders can often fall into the trap of asking the coach to work with the ineffective teacher as a "fix" or a consequence for a subpar observation. Or the principal may even ask the teacher to set up a time to meet with the coach. Both scenarios are reactive in nature and may occur before the coach establishes him- or herself as a copartner and collaborator. Additionally, the teacher's performance could so dismay or anger both the principal and the coach that they channel all their energy into punishing the teacher, for example by putting a teacher on a formal improvement plan or passively changing his or her grade-level assignment. I've seen that these negative reactions and strong emotions toward the teacher only add fuel to the fire, and any punishment will at best force compliance from a teacher. It certainly won't change teacher efficacy or student learning.

We have an opportunity to harness and direct these emotions and this negative energy in a more constructive way by placing our focus on supporting students, rather than on punishing or criticizing teachers. In chapter 4 (page 37), we explored how our discourse changes the nature of our dialogue and the nature of the coach-teacher relationship. In keeping with effective discourse, when approaching a teacher, the coach can frame comments and questions to focus on the student outcomes that teacher actions can inspire. This practice de-emphasizes the idea of working with an ineffective teacher and instead focuses the work on effective student learning. Table 7.1 features comparisons between teacher-centered conversation frames and student-centered conversation frames. The left column of this table lists questions that coaches traditionally ask when addressing a teacher after they have observed a lesson, while the right column contains alternative suggestions to shift conventional questions to transformative ones.

**Table 7.1: Conversation Frames**

| Teacher-Centered, Low-Teacher-Inspiration Questions | Student-Centered, High-Teacher-Inspiration Questions |
|---|---|
| "How do you think the lesson went?" | "Did your students learn at high levels, and how do you know?" |
| "What could you have done better?" | "What are some innovative ways we could support students to shift their thinking?" |
| "What will you do differently next time?" | "How will you and your students reflect on the learning that occurred?" |
| "What were your favorite parts of the lesson?" | "Where did you see the light bulb come on for students? At what points did you hear joy in their voice or laughter, or see a smile?" |
| "What are your strengths?" | "Where are your students' strengths, and how do you support them in building their strengths?" |

The questions on the right side not only focus on the student perspective but also prompt teachers to reflect on and then proactively begin to ponder their own beliefs about their perceived efficacy. The coach is essential in supporting the teacher in moving from reflection to action, which they accomplish through reverberation cycles (see chapter 5, page 50). The teacher metacognitively reflects on his or her own learning regarding student practice in tandem with his or her own pedagogical practice, behaviors, and strategies. As a coach continually frames questions in this way, he or she aims to have teachers continually reframe how they view themselves and to inspire intrinsically motivated actions that do what's best for students. In turn, a change in teacher practice and efficacy influences student learning and growth.

# Getting Divergent Ideas to Fly

Change often requires lofty goals and paradigm shifts. It requires educators to engage in divergent thinking to generate many different ideas about an issue in hopes of gaining insight about the various aspects of the issue. These divergent ideas deviate from the norm and challenge conventional thinking. Divergent thinking and divergent ideas provide a means to an end: to change behaviors, look at something through a new lens, or completely unhinge a paradigm. Coaches play an influential role in getting divergent ideas to fly and changing paradigms. However, unhinging a paradigm can unhinge teachers' nerves. Divergent thinking and divergent ideas are often antithetical to existing knowledge and intuition. Grant (2016) offers two strategies for encouraging divergent thinking and making divergent ideas more palatable: (1) couching and (2) repositioning. I've identified a third strategy that also supports faculty reception of divergent ideas: championing dissenters over cheerleaders. These three strategies support coaches in building and leveraging influence as they help teachers with the difficult task of change.

## Couching Ideas in Existing Conventions

Grant (2016) states that instead of trying to change people's minds, we can appeal to values or beliefs that those people already hold. So in the case of countering intuition, we can often couch divergent ideas in more conventional methods that teachers feel comfortable with. For example, when I worked as an administrator, my fellow district leaders wanted to change the teacher practice of simply writing a lesson's related content standard on the board to creating a meaningful student-friendly learning target that was an integral part of the lesson. When I looked at the end goal, I found it deviated from current practice. We wanted not to solely create buy-in but to truly instill in teachers the belief that this new practice would enhance the focus, clarity, and motivation of the lesson, and therefore enhance learning.

As part of creating this belief, we needed to hook the new practice to something that was already part of current practice (couch this new idea in something conventional): writing down the content standard. Our messaging signified that we were already providing a general purpose of the lesson, so now, we would start with what we already did and build on it. We successfully implemented student-friendly learning targets because we couched them in a previously conventional practice of writing content standards and showed teachers they were already on their way to the new change.

## Repositioning the Change Initiative

Grant (2016) also provides advice to reposition the change initiative or idea as a means to an end that matters to others. *Repositioning* is approaching a concept from a different angle in hopes of making a more meaningful connection. For example, I once worked with a teacher who didn't assign homework. I lauded her apparent focus on providing meaningful learning experiences, instead of pursuing compliance and unconnected busywork. As I sought more information, I learned that this lack of homework resulted from her improvisational teaching style and her time constraints for grading homework, and not from a philosophical belief. I gravitated toward her visible methods, not her reasoning or beliefs (or lack thereof) behind them. We didn't share in the purpose and the *why*. Even though she had a different *why*, I could leverage this scenario to inspire change in the school culture. With a goal of shifting from compliance-based homework to meaningful and value-added student work in our school culture, this teacher could be the first to make this shift in thinking.

Her methods and the *how* already aligned with this vision, so the change had a lesser magnitude for her. She became one of the first allies and influencers for change in this effort because in my conversations with her I repositioned the issue of homework as something that benefits teachers (time saver, less arduous work, and so on). Homework reduction had success in this scenario because we repositioned it for a teacher who was already doing what the change called for. The teacher became an ally for change and helped showcase how a reduction of homework results in higher student motivation and more meaningful student learning experiences.

The tool in figure 7.1 can help in determining a coach's approach for getting divergent ideas to fly. It illustrates Grant's (2016) two strategic pathways for promoting divergent ideas and converting them into shared buy-in and action.

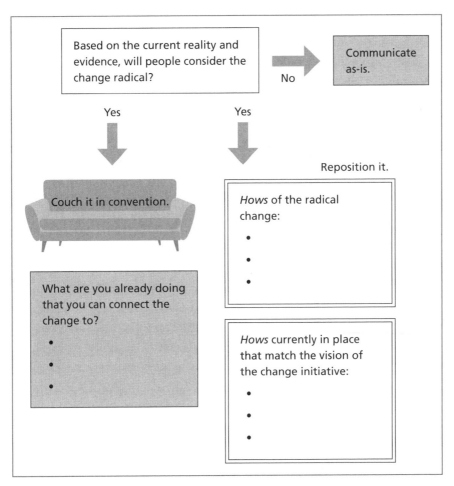

**Figure 7.1: Pathways-to-divergence tool.**

Where do instructional coaches fit into this? Because of the nature of the work and the role of instructional coaches, they can provide a comprehensive picture of the current reality in their building. They can help the school leaders decide on the magnitude of change (how radical it is) and if they can connect it to current practices (couch it) or reposition it in order to help teachers see how their existing practices can facilitate the change. Instructional coaches truly partner with administrators to shift paradigms together and champion divergent ideas.

## Championing Dissenters Over Cheerleaders

It may seem logical that if a coach wants to induce change throughout an organization, he or she should begin by gaining the buy-in of the organization's known cheerleaders. Then the cheerleaders will loudly and positively spread the message, inspiring others to jump on board. The problem with this approach is that everyone else in the building has likely already caught on to the notion that these cheerleaders will always champion whatever the principal or coach asks of the staff. People in the building begin to consider this cheerleading a charade and think, "They can't possibly think this is a good idea; they love every idea that comes down the pike."

Continually tapping into cheerleaders encourages *groupthink*, which *Oxford Dictionaries* (n.d.) defines as "the practice of thinking or making decisions as a group in a way that discourages creativity or individual responsibility." This prevents genuine change from taking place. (See chapter 1, page 12, for a discussion of groupthink.) Further, psychologist Irving Janis (1972) determines that groupthink promotes an unhealthy culture of decision making. While many school leaders first seek support for divergent ideas from the cheerleaders, paradoxically, this is detrimental. A more effective place to start is with dissenters.

Seeing consistent dissenters embodying a new concept could encourage others to seriously question their own hesitations about the concept. For example, I once worked with a teacher, who later became an instructional coach, who seemed to pick out flaws or problems in every plan and initiative. People in the school quickly labeled her a complainer who just didn't want to put forth the work to make the plans happen. But as I developed a relationship with this soon-to-be coach, I discovered her brilliance, healthy work ethic, and positivity and that, in reality, when dissenters go against the grain, they can continually find important weak spots and holes in the plans they question. I decided that I would always go to her and other dissenting teachers when I had a newly formed divergent idea. They could scrutinize it and in the end make it better. Once an idea went through their stringent criticism, then the dissenters championed change, and I had more confidence that this divergent idea would fly. The dissenters were the champions of change. School leaders need dissenters who understand the change and would be willing to change, but need the weak spots to be acknowledged before they can advocate for and participate in the change.

Ideas can become better if dissenters, instead of cheerleaders, first champion them. Dissenters are able to illuminate the strong parts of the change and identify the weak parts.

Some of the best coaches I've seen have been dissenters. If you aren't naturally a dissenter, don't worry—you don't have to personify some negative shadow of yourself. But you can always question whether you have a better way to do something, and you can always seek out scrutiny and support from dissenting teachers. Coaches who form close relationships with teachers can play a pivotal role in identifying dissenters and existing preconceptions in the collective teaching staff. When coaches build mutual respect and trust with these dissenters as well as the principal and other teachers, they can leverage divergent ideas and achieve successful implementation.

## Moving Forward Through the Unknown

Changing a belief system or a paradigm doesn't happen like flipping a switch. It often happens when we experience a *black swan event*. What is a black swan event? Essayist and scholar Nassim Nicholas Taleb (2007) conceptualizes this metaphor to describe an occurrence that falls outside the realm of typical expectations, carries an extreme impact, and gets explained and made predictable after the fact. Taleb (2007) claims, "A small number of black swans explain almost everything in our world, from the success of ideas and religions, to the dynamics of historical events, to elements of our own personal lives" (p. xxii).

One example of a black swan event in education might be a district's receipt of unexpectedly low test scores on a new assessment that the local district or the state created. The building principal and instructional coach immediately begin to reason through why the students received surprisingly low scores. They may conclude that the newly designed assessment can explain the low scores and that students weren't prepared for the assessment because their learning opportunities didn't align with how the test assessed them. Or school leaders may conclude that a lack of fidelity to a consistent and sound instructional framework in the building explains the results. These conclusions begin to affect the lens through which school leadership sees future events and outcomes related to this particular event. School leaders' paradigm has shifted. With this new narrative in place, they tell themselves they could have, and perhaps should have, anticipated this black swan event, and the administrative team builds an action plan to curb the negative circumstances (low student achievement) surrounding the event.

In this case, the leadership focuses on the event itself and its outcomes. As coaches, we've come to understand the consequences of forming hard and fast conclusions on evidence. We may later come to the conclusion that the test items actually were not well designed or that they did not closely relate to innovative real-world classroom practices. The point is that we see the fragility in our processes and acknowledge that we may create binders full of action plans or change our vision, only to have it changed again when an unexpected event occurs.

Highlighting historical examples and making connections to educators' current reality can provide a powerful context for divergent ideas. It allows us as educators to accept the unpredictable nature of the world we live in, and we learn to adapt to this nature by taking risks and thinking in new ways. We conclude that not the ideas themselves but the process of embodying a new type of thinking may transform our practice.

However, as we move to transform these new, divergent ideas into actions, many teachers may struggle with jumping into the unknown due to the pressures and accountability measures that are in place in schools. One fear that often resounds is, "Will this new change have any consequence on my principal's evaluation, my coach's support of me, or test scores tied to my evaluation score?" How do we support teachers' practice in the context of the unknown? The following recommendations provide some guidance.

- **Consistent affirmation of progress:** Coaches provide consistent support by affirming the great work teachers have always done, and they point out the fact that teachers have come this far, so they can't stop now.

- **Lateral empathy:** Coaches work under similar accountability measures as teachers do; therefore, lateral empathy can build trust and confidence in the coach-teacher relationship as they face the unknown together.

- **Backward reflection:** Even though teachers are often concerned about how the consequences of change efforts may affect the perceived or actual effectiveness of their efforts, if teachers reflect back, they would be hard-pressed to find times when changes have actually burned them.

Figure 7.2 provides an example of a tool that can support coaches in their work with teachers to implement new ideas and help them address the anxiety or fear of failure that comes with trying something different. In this example, the teacher reflects on the change of moving away from assigning traditional letter grades. Working through this divergence-reflection tool with the teacher helps highlight how he or she has previously embraced divergent ideas that are a part of change initiatives.

Building leaders who partner with instructional coaches can create a culture of embracing the possibility of the unexpected and coping with one of our greatest fears: change. Coaches should strive to embody this principle as they work with teachers, exposing their vulnerability by acknowledging their fears and uncertainties about the future, but continually pushing forward for the sake of growth for the teaching profession and student learning.

| Past Divergent Idea | How You Felt in the Beginning | Student Successes | How You Felt After the Student Successes |
|---|---|---|---|
| Eliminate letter grades and move to a focus on formative assessment and feedback. | I was very skeptical at first. I felt like it was another new fad to adopt. Students and parents are very accustomed to receiving letter grades. Some students will work harder if they know they can get an A or they fear getting a lower grade. | Students were confused by the change at first. But over time, the feedback became more transformative and meaningful than a letter grade. The data we collected and the kind of feedback provided empowered students to take ownership, and therefore, they became proud of their work, and that provided more motivation than a letter grade. | I felt inspired as a teacher and facilitator of learning. I can't imagine going back to giving letter grades. |
|  |  |  |  |
|  |  |  |  |
|  |  |  |  |

**Figure 7.2: Divergence-reflection tool example.**

*Visit **go.SolutionTree.com/instruction** for a free reproducible version of this figure.*

## Conclusion

When implementing change, coaches should focus on the *how* as they continually remind themselves of the *why*, the *what*, and the *where*—*where* do they want students to be as a result of the *why*? Change is more effective if the *why*, *what*, and *where* have been clearly established before diving into the nuts and bolts of the *how*. Coaches can act as positive forces and influencers of change if they take purposeful actions that work to disband ineffective teaching and instructional practices, reframing the focus from ineffective teachers to effective student learning practices. This laser focus provides a new schema for teachers to change their actions for the sake of student growth. Coaches can also leverage fear of the unknown and its resulting fragility to inspire change through consistent acknowledgment of progress, lateral empathy, and a reflection of past divergent ideas that eventually became transformational actions. They can work to ensure positive reception of change initiatives by embracing dissenters' criticism, rather than winning over cheerleaders who routinely accept ideas with automaticity. Working with dissenters to address their concerns, and enlisting their support for an initiative, will influence others to consider and work toward making changes with an open mind.

Because coaches approach relationships with teachers from a nonevaluative stance, it inherently increases their credibility and influence and dismantles any defense mechanisms that the coach and the teacher may have present between them. The coach has more opportunities to support a shared vision at the classroom level and observe activities that may not align with the vision. This provides opportunities for the coach to ask questions to gain a better understanding of why the vision-action gaps exist, and to partner with the teacher to work collaboratively toward the agreed-on goals.

# EPILOGUE

Creating meaningful change is an ongoing journey that involves open-mindedness, continual reflection, and engagement in personal and professional learning. With the seven drivers of instructional coaching, we can transform teaching and learning, but not unless a school community culture values these drivers, which instructional coaches are pivotal in influencing. We shouldn't view coaching as a quick fix or even a solution to change anyone. If teachers change, they do so not because a coach has changed them; they do so because they want to change. We should view coaching as a powerful support system to help teachers and students think, learn, collaborate, and create in new and previously unimagined ways. Consequently, this support begins to influence a teacher's belief system about his or her own practice, with a change in behaviors following suit. When an instructional coach clearly articulates his or her mission and puts drivers for success into practice daily, instructional coaching can begin to deliver on the promise of being a game changer in education.

An old saying goes, "We don't know what we don't know." Educators need an outside perspective that allows them to see things in the classroom they don't know exist regarding instruction and treatment of students, because they stay so busy and focused on teaching that they cannot see all that happens or read their students' minds (DeWitt, 2014). This truth can also apply to coaching, as coaches also need someone to help them see things from another perspective, just as teachers do. In her TED Talks, novelist Chimamanda Adichie (2009) tells the story of how she found her authentic cultural voice, and in doing so, she reveals how our lives and our cultures are composed of many overlapping stories, not just a single story or perspective. If we hear only a single story or view of the world based on a static narrative, we risk critically misunderstanding others' worldviews, behaviors, and actions. As coaches navigate change and employ the drivers in this book, they will begin to bring in multiple perspectives and diverse viewpoints, crafting an educational worldview that's open, dynamic, unbiased, and inclusive. This approach creates conditions primed for meaningful engagement, creativity, innovation, and transformation not only for the craft of instructional coaching but also for the culture of teaching and learning across the globe.

# REFERENCES AND RESOURCES

Adichie, C. N. (2009, July). *The danger of a single story* [Video file]. Accessed at www.ted.com/talks/chimamanda_adichie_the_danger_of_a_single_story /transcript?language=en on August 30, 2017.

Avolio, B. J., Gardner, W. L., Walumbwa, F. O., Luthans, F., & May, D. R. (2004). Unlocking the mask: A look at the process by which authentic leaders impact follower attitudes and behaviors. *The Leadership Quarterly, 15*(6), 801–823.

Bandura, A. (1977). Self-efficacy: Toward a unifying theory of behavioral change. *Psychological Review, 84*(2), 191–215.

Beck, D. E., & Cowan, C. C. (1996). *Spiral dynamics: Mastering values, leadership, and change.* Cambridge, MA: Blackwell Business.

Bendersky, C., & Shah, N. P. (2013). The downfall of extraverts and rise of neurotics: The dynamic process of status allocation in task groups. *Academy of Management Journal, 56*(2), 387–406.

Berger, W. (2014). *A more beautiful question: The power of inquiry to spark breakthrough ideas.* New York: Bloomsbury USA.

Brown, C. B. (2010). *The gifts of imperfection: Let go of who you think you're supposed to be and embrace who you are.* Center City, MN: Hazelden.

Cain, S. (2012, February). *The power of introverts* [Video file]. Accessed at www .ted.com/talks/susan_cain_the_power_of_introverts on August 30, 2017.

Cain, S. (2013). *Quiet: The power of introverts in a world that can't stop talking.* New York: Broadway Paperbacks.

Černe, M., Jaklič, M., & Škerlavaj, M. (2013). Authentic leadership, creativity, and innovation: A multilevel perspective. *Leadership, 9*(1), 63–85.

Daggett, W. R., & Jones, R. D. (2014). *The process of change: Why change, what to do, and how to do it.* Rexford, NY: International Center for Leadership in Education. Accessed at www.leadered.com/pdf/Process_of_Change_2014.pdf on August 31, 2017.

DeWitt, P. (2014, November 6). Five reasons we need instructional coaches. *Education Week.* Accessed at http://blogs.edweek.org/edweek/finding _common_ground/2014/11/5_reasons_we_need_instructional_coaches .html on August 31, 2017.

DeWitt, P., & Lang, N. D. (2016, May 26). Why our feedback is backfiring. *Education Week.* Accessed at http://blogs.edweek.org/edweek /finding_common_ground/2016/05/why_our_feedback_is_backfiring.html on August 30, 2017.

Drucker, P. F. (2008). *The five most important questions you will ever ask about your organization.* San Francisco: Jossey-Bass.

Dutton, J. E. (2003). *Energize your workplace: How to create and sustain high-quality connections at work.* San Francisco: Jossey-Bass.

Dweck, C. S. (2007). The perils and promises of praise. *Educational Leadership, 65*(2), 34–39.

Fast, N. J., Burris, E. R., & Bartel, C. A. (2014). Managing to stay in the dark: Managerial self-efficacy, ego defensiveness, and the aversion to employee voice. *Academy of Management Journal, 57*(4), 1013–1034.

Fragale, A. R. (2006). The power of powerless speech: The effects of speech style and task interdependence on status conferral. *Organizational Behavior and Human Decision Processes, 101*(2), 243–261.

Gangestad, S. W., & Snyder, M. (2000). Self-monitoring: Appraisal and reappraisal. *Psychological Bulletin, 126*(4), 530–555.

Ghose, T. (2013, February 6). Why we're all above average. *Live Science.* Accessed at www.livescience.com/26914-why-we-are-all-above-average.html on August 31, 2017.

Godin, S. (2012). *Stop stealing dreams: What is school for?* Accessed at www .sethgodin.com/sg/docs/stopstealingdreamsscreen.pdf on August 31, 2017.

Grant, A. (2014). *Give and take: Why helping others drives our success.* New York: Penguin Books.

Grant, A. (2016). *Originals: How non-conformists move the world.* New York: Penguin Books.

Grant, A., Gino, F., & Hofmann, D. A. (2010). The hidden advantages of quiet bosses. *Harvard Business Review.* Accessed at https://hbr.org/2010/12/the -hidden-advantages-of-quiet-bosses on August 30, 2017.

Graves, C. W., & Lee, W. R. (2004). *Levels of human existence: Transcription of a seminar at the Washington School of Psychiatry, October 16, 1971.* Santa Barbara, CA: ECLET.

Groupthink. (n.d.). In *Oxford Dictionaries online*. Accessed at https://en.oxforddictionaries.com/definition/us/groupthink on October 12, 2017.

Hattie, J. (2015). *What doesn't work in education: The politics of distraction*. London: Pearson. Accessed at https://visible-learning.org/wp-content/uploads/2015/06/John-Hattie-Visible-Learning-creative-commons-book-free-PDF-download-What-doesn-t-work-in-education_the-politics-of-distraction-pearson-2015.pdf on August 30, 2017.

Hattie, J., & Timperley, H. (2007). The power of feedback. *Review of Educational Research, 77*(1), 81–112.

Hattie, J., & Yates, G. C. R. (2014). Using feedback to promote learning. In V. A. Benassi, C. E. Overson, & C. M. Hakala (Eds.), *Applying science of learning in education: Infusing psychological science into the curriculum* (pp. 45–58). Accessed at http://teachpsych.org/Resources/Documents/ebooks/asle2014.pdf on September 28, 2017.

Heathfield, S. M. (2016, August 14). *360 degree feedback: The good, the bad and the ugly—What is 360 degree feedback?* Accessed at www.thebalance.com/360-degree-feedback-information-1917537 on August 30, 2017.

Holiday, R. (2016). *Ego is the enemy*. New York: Portfolio.

Hudgens, L. H. (2016, May 26). Do teachers care more about schoolwork than your kids do? Here's how to fix the apathy problem. *The Washington Post*. Accessed at www.washingtonpost.com/news/parenting/wp/2016/05/26/do-teachers-care-more-about-your-kids-schoolwork-than-they-do-how-to-fix-the-apathy-problem/?utm_term=.ee30c4e0be38 on November 13, 2017.

Innes, R. B. (2007). Dialogic communication in collaborative problem solving groups. *International Journal for the Scholarship of Teaching and Learning, 1*(1), 4.

Janis, I. L. (1972). *Victims of groupthink: A psychological study of foreign-policy decisions and fiascoes*. Boston: Houghton Mifflin.

Jensen, S. M., & Luthans, F. (2006). Relationship between entrepreneurs' psychological capital and their authentic leadership. *Journal of Managerial Issues, 18*(2), 254–273.

Keltner, D., Gruenfeld, D. H., & Anderson, C. (2003). Power, approach, and inhibition. *Psychological Review, 110*(2), 265–284.

Kirwan Institute for the Study of Race and Ethnicity. (2015). *Understanding implicit bias*. Accessed at http://kirwaninstitute.osu.edu/research/understanding-implicit-bias on January 24, 2018.

Knight, J. (2007). *Instructional coaching: A partnership approach to improving instruction*. Thousand Oaks, CA: Corwin Press.

Knight, J. (2010). *Unmistakable impact: A partnership approach for dramatically improving instruction*. Thousand Oaks, CA: Corwin Press.

Kounin, J. S. (1970). *Discipline and group management in classrooms.* New York: Holt, Rinehart and Winston.

Kruger, J., & Dunning, D. (1999). Unskilled and unaware of it: How difficulties in recognizing one's own incompetence lead to inflated self-assessments. *Journal of Personality and Social Psychology, 77*(6), 1121–1134.

Lencioni, P. M. (2010). *Getting naked: A business fable about shedding the three fears that sabotage client loyalty.* San Francisco: Jossey-Bass.

Lev-Ari, S., & Keysar, B. (2010). Why don't we believe non-native speakers? The influence of accent on credibility. *Journal of Experimental Social Psychology, 46*(6), 1093–1096.

Locke, E. A., Cartledge, N., & Knerr, C. S. (1970). Studies of the relationship between satisfaction, goal-setting, and performance. *Organizational Behavior and Human Performance, 5*(2), 135–158.

Novicevic, M. M., Davis, W., Dorn, F., Buckley, M. R., & Brown, J. A. (2005). Barnard on conflicts of responsibility: Implications for today's perspectives on transformational and authentic leadership. *Management Decision, 43*(10), 1396–1409.

Nuthall, G. (n.d.). *Classroom discourse.* Accessed at http://education .stateuniversity.com/pages/1916/Discourse.html on August 30, 2017.

Partnership for 21st Century Skills. (2011). *Framework for 21st century learning.* Accessed at www.p21.org/storage/documents/1.__p21_framework_2-pager .pdf on October 12, 2017.

Peterson, S. J., & Luthans, F. (2003). The positive impact and development of hopeful leaders. *Leadership and Organization Development Journal, 24*(1), 26–31.

Phillips, K. W., Mannix, E. A., Neale, M. A., & Gruenfeld, D. H. (2004). Diverse groups and information sharing: The effects of congruent ties. *Journal of Experimental Social Psychology, 40*(4), 497–510.

Quaglia Institute for School Voice and Aspirations. (n.d.). *Quaglia school voice model.* Accessed at http://quagliainstitute.org/qisva/library /schoolVoiceModel.jsp on August 31, 2017.

Quaglia Institute for School Voice and Aspirations. (2016). *The aspirations framework.* Accessed at http://quagliainstitute.org/dmsView/Aspirations _Framework on February 23, 2018.

Rhodes, J. (n.d.). Why do I think better after I exercise? *Scientific American.* Accessed at www.scientificamerican.com/article/why-do-you-think-better -after-walk-exercise on November 13, 2017.

Right Question Institute. (n.d.). *Experiencing the question formulation technique.* Accessed at www.ibmidatlantic.org/Experiencing-the-QFT.pdf on October 12, 2017.

Right Question Institute. (2017). *Educator resource area*. Accessed at http://
rightquestion.org/educators/resources on August 31, 2017.

Roemischer, J. (2002). The never-ending upward quest. *What Is Enlightenment?*,
*22*, 1–24. Accessed at www.mcs-international.org/downloads/046
_spiraldynamics_wie.pdf on October 12, 2017.

Rose, J. (2012, May 9). How to break free of our 19th-century factory-model
education system. *The Atlantic*. Accessed at www.theatlantic.com/business
/archive/2012/05/how-to-break-free-of-our-19th-century-factory-model
-education-system/256881 on November 13, 2017.

Ross, H. J. (2014). *Everyday bias: Identifying and navigating unconscious judgments
in our daily lives*. Lanham, MD: Rowman & Littlefield.

Rothstein, D., Santana, L., & Minigan, A. P. (2015). Making questions flow.
*Educational Leadership*, *73*(1), 70–75.

Sackstein, S. (2016, January 5). Passion projects ignite student interest.
*Education Week*. Accessed at http://blogs.edweek.org/teachers/work_in
_progress/2016/01/passion_projects_ignite_studen.html?override=web on
October 9, 2017.

Sackstein, S., & Lang, N. D. (2016, October 23). Why passion isn't enough.
*Education Week*. Accessed at http://blogs.edweek.org/teachers/work
_in_progress/2016/10/why_passion_isnt_enough.html on October 9, 2017.

Sinek, S. (2009). *Start with why: How great leaders inspire everyone to take action*.
New York: Portfolio.

Staats, C. (2016). Understanding implicit bias: What educators should know.
*American Educator*, *39*(4), 29–33, 43.

Taleb, N. N. (2007). *The black swan: The impact of the highly improbable*. New
York: Random House.

Wiggins, G. (2010, March 27). *What is transfer?* Accessed at
www.authenticeducation.org/ae_bigideas/article.lasso?artid=60 on October
9, 2017.

Wilber, K. (2006). *Integral spirituality: A startling new role for religion in the
modern and postmodern world*. Boston: Integral Books.

Wozniak, S. (2007). *iWoz: Computer geek to cult icon—How I invented the
personal computer, co-founded Apple, and had fun doing it*. New York: Norton.

Zaki, J., & Ochsner, K. N. (2012). The neuroscience of empathy: Progress,
pitfalls and promise. *Nature Neuroscience*, *15*(5), 675–680.

# INDEX